CHINE
PC

A Headway phrasebook

Yang Yujie

Headway · Hodder & Stoughton

*The author and publishers would like to thank Ms
Guilan Wang for her meticulous checking of all the
materials, and for her kind help and advice throughout.*

British Library Cataloguing in Publication Data
Yang, Yujie
   Chinese in your pocket. – (A Headway phrasebook).
   1. Chinese language. Usage
   I. Title
   495.18

   ISBN 0 340 51846 4

First published 1991

Typeset by Graphicraft Typesetters Ltd., Hong Kong.
Printed in Hong Kong for the educational publishing division
of Hodder and Stoughton Ltd, Mill Road, Dunton Green,
Sevenoaks, Kent by Colorcraft Ltd.

Contents

Introduction

China is becoming an increasingly popular destination with Western holidaymakers and business travellers alike. However, travelling to China is often a much more daunting prospect than travelling to other countries. The language, culture and way of thinking are very different to those in western countries, and this often prevents visitors from making the most of their stay in China. *Chinese in your Pocket* aims to overcome some of these differences, particularly in language and culture, enabling you to communicate and to feel more comfortable in this unique society.

The book covers everyday situations which you are likely to encounter, giving phrases in both Chinese characters and *pīnyīn* (the official Chinese phonetics system), so that if you fail to make yourself understood, you can simply point to the phrase in question. Special 'You may hear' sections are provided so that you can understand what is being said by asking the person to point to the appropriate phrase in the book. Although there are many dialects in China, Mandarin Chinese is the official language and will be understood in most places. All phrases in this book, therefore, use modern Mandarin Chinese. It would be a good idea to study the Pronunciation and Basic Expressions first (see pages 5 and 8) to familiarise yourself with the sounds of Chinese and a few simple words before attempting to use the main phrase sections.

The Chinese will be flattered and delighted that you have made an effort to speak their language, and you will get much more out of your trip to China

一路顺风!

Pronunciation

As mentioned in the introduction, all phrases in this book are given in both *pīnyīn* and Chinese characters. *Pīnyīn* is the official system for transcribing the Chinese language using the Latin (ie our) alphabet.

Each Chinese character represents a syllable rather than a letter, and consists of 'initials' and 'finals' (which can be likened to our consonants and vowels and are explained more fully on page 6). The meaning of a word, however, is determined by its tone. This means the pitch at which a word or syllable is spoken. There are four basic tones in Chinese:

- ¯ 1st tone (high) is spoken at quite a high pitch, and neither falls or rises.
- ´ 2nd tone (rising) rises from a middle to high pitch.
- ˇ 3rd tone (falling–rising) goes from middle to low to high.
- ` 4th tone (falling) goes from high to low pitch.

The figure below illustrates the four tones:

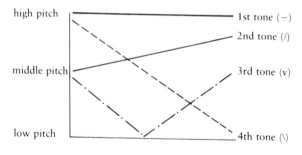

Thus *mǎi* means 'buy' but *mài* means 'sell'.

táng means 'sugar' but *tāng* means 'soup'.

So you can see that tone is very important when pronouncing Chinese. The above symbols are used throughout this book to indicate tone: if there is no tone mark, the syllable is unstressed and is pronounced with a neutral tone.

Sometimes a character is pronounced with different tones without changing the meaning. For example, the numeral ¯ *yī* (one) is pronounced in the first tone when it stands alone, or in counting, in the fourth tone when followed by a first, second or third tone syllable and in the second tone when followed by a fourth tone syllable.

一二	one, two
yī èr	
一张饼	one pancake
yì zhāng bǐng	
一盘菜	one dish
yì pán cài	
一本书	one book
yì běn shū	
一个人	one person
yí gè rén	

When two third tones occur together in spoken Chinese, the first one is generally pronounced as a second tone. That is why the character 我 (I, me) is sometimes shown as *wǒ* and sometimes as *wó*. Where a word is composed of more that one character, the syllables in *pīnyīn* are run together to make a single word. For example 中国 (China) is written as *zhōngguó*, and not as *zhōng guó* or *zhōng-guó*.

Initials and Finals (vowels and consonants)

The only way to achieve accurate pronunciation is to find a native speaker, but the following guidelines will enable you to make yourself understood, as most Chinese sounds can be approximated to English vowels and consonants. The main differences are listed below:

Initials

c   like 'ts' in 'cats', followed by a strong puff of breath
ch like 'ch' in 'church', but with the tip of the tongue turned to touch the roof of the mouth
g   like 'g' in 'girl'
h   like 'ch' in Scottish 'loch'
j   like 'j' in 'jeer', pronounced very near the front of the mouth

q   lik 'ch' in 'bench', but with the tip of the tongue
       against the lower teeth
r   a cross between English 'r' and the 's' in 'pleasure'
x   like 'sh' in 'she' but with the lips widely spread
z   like 'ds' in 'kids'
zh like 'j' in 'jug', but with the tip of the tongue turned
       to touch the roof of the mouth

Finals

a   like 'a' in 'car' (without the 'r')
e   like 'e' in 'her' (without the 'r')
i   *after 'c', 's', 'z', 'ch', 'sh', 'zh' and 'r': like 'e' in
         'her' (without the 'r')
         *elsewhere: like 'ee' in 'flee'
ian like 'yen'
o   like 'aw' in 'saw'
ong like 'ong' in 'wrong', but with a rounder mouth
u   like 'oo' in 'spoon'
ü   like the German 'ü': say 'ee' with the lips rounded
         (only occurs after 'n' or 'l')
ue   like 'oo-eh', but pronounced as one syllable
(üe) after 'n' or 'l')
ui   like 'way'
un   like 'one', but pronounced 'win' after 'j', 'q' and 'x'

There are various other diphthongs and triphthongs in
Chinese. They are all pronounced as one syllable with
the various elements gliding into one another.

Basic Expressions

yes	} see Grammar section
no	} page 12
please	请
	qǐng
thank you	谢谢
	xièxie
thank you very much	太谢谢您了
	tài xièxie nín le
hello	喂
	wèi
How are you?	你好吗？
	Ní hǎo ma
Excuse me (I'm sorry)	对不起
	Duìbùqǐ
(to get attention)	劳驾!
	Láojià!
(to get past)	借光
	Jièguāng
Don't mention it	不(用)谢
	Bú (yòng) xiè
I'm sorry I'm late	我很抱歉。来晚了
	Wó hěn bàoqiàn. Lái wǎn le
It doesn't matter	没什么
	Méi shénme
Just a minute	等一下
	Děng yíxià
Do you speak English?	你会说英语吗？
	Nǐ huì shuō yīngyǔ ma?
Could you point to the phrase in the book?	请指给我是哪几个字？
	Qǐng zhǐgei wǒ shì nǎ jǐge zì?
I (don't) understand	我(不)懂
	Wǒ (bù) dǒng
Goodbye	再见
	Zàijiàn
Ladies	女厕所
	nǚcèsuǒ

Basic Expressions

Gents   男厕所
                              Náncèsuǒ

● It is important that you familiarise yourself with the last two, as Chinese public toilets are usually indicated by characters alone, sometimes with pinyin.

Forms of Address

先生 *xiānsheng*	sir	夫人/太太 *fūren/tàitai*	madam
小姐 *xiǎojie*	miss	女士 *nǚshi*	ms
同志 *tóngzhì*	comrade	师傅 *shīfu*	master/skilled worker

● The first four of these were condemned as 'bourgeois' during the Cultural Revolution, but nowadays they can be used freely on formal occasions.
● Chinese people tend to use the bottom two titles frequently amongst themselves, and, as a guest in China, you can use *shīfu* in public places when addressing a stranger. In intellectual circles, the title 老师 *lǎoshī* (teacher) can be used.
All these titles come *after* the name, not before it as in English.
● Titles are used as polite forms of address as the equivalent of 'you'. So you might say 先生，您好吗？ *Xiānshēng, nín hǎo ma?* (Sir, are you well?) or simply 先生，好吗？ *Xiānshēng, hǎo ma?* (Is the gentleman well?).

Chinese Names

The order for Chinese names is surname and then first name. In a three-character name, the first is the surname and the second two are the first name. Because of this difference between Western and Chinese usage, you may find yourself addressed by a title followed by your first name. Women in China do not change their surname after marriage, so if you are unsure of a woman's status, it is safer to use *nǚshi* (or *xiǎojie* for a younger woman).

Basic Expressions

Greetings

For most school and university students, English is a compulsory subject and most are eager to try out their English on native speakers. Some of their phrases, however, might sound a bit odd, because direct translations of traditional Chinese greetings result in such phrases as 'Where are you going?', 'What are you doing here?' or 'Have you had your breakfast?'. These forms are the equivalent of 'How do you do?' or 'How are you?' in English, and should not be taken too personally.

You may hear:	
你是 ... 先生吗？ *Nǐ shì ... xiānsheng ma?*	**Are you Mr ...?**
你是 ... 小姐吗？ *Nǐ shì ... xiǎojie ma?*	**Are you Miss ...?**

Yes, I am	我是 *Wǒ shì*
No, I am not	我不是 *Wǒ búshì*

You may hear:	
你是哪国人？ *Nǐ shì nǎ guó rén?*	**What nationality are you?**
你上哪去？ *Nǐ shàng nǎ qù?*	**Where are you going?**
你在这做什么？ *Nǐ zài zhè zuò shénme?*	**What are you doing here?**
你第一次来中国吗？ *Nǐ dì yícì lái Zhōngguó ma?*	**Is it your first visit to China?**
我能帮你吗？ *Wǒ néng bāng nǐ ma?*	**May I help you?**

Basic Expressions

I'm ...	我是 ... *Wǒ shì ...*
... British	英国人 *... Yīngguó rén*
... Irish	爱尔兰人 *... Ài'ěrlán rén*
... American	美国人 *... Měiguó rén*
... Canadian	加拿大人 *... Jiānádà rén*
... Australian	澳大利亚人 *... Àodàlìyà rén*
... New Zealander	新西兰人 *... Xīnxīlán rén*

- Chinese names of countries are usually formed with the syllable 国 *guó*, meaning 'country'. *Zhōngguó* (China) is made up of two syllables: *zhóng* (middle) and *gúo* (country or kingdom). This reflects the ancient notion that China was the centre of the universe.
- *Zhōngwén* originally referred to Chinese writing, but is now used more generally for the Chinese language. 中文书 *Zhōngwénshū* refers specifically to a book in the Chinese language, whereas *Zhōngguóshū*, which might just mean a book published in China.

How do you do? (formal)	您好 *Nín hǎo*
How do you do? (informal)	你好 *Nǐ hǎo*
Pleased to meet you	见到你很高兴 *Jiàndào nǐ hěn gāoxìng*
I do not speak (Chinese/English)	我不会说中文/英语 *Wǒ búhuì shuō* *(Zhōngwén/Yīngyǔ)*

Basic Expressions

Do you speak (Chinese/English)?

你会讲中文/英语吗？

Nǐ huìjiǎng (Zhōngwén/Yīngyǔ) ma?

A little

一点儿

Yìdiǎnr

Please speak more slowly

请讲慢点

Qǐng jiǎng màn diǎn

I don't understand

我不懂

Wǒ bùdǒng

What does it mean?

什么意思？

Shénme yìsi?

How do you say ... in Chinese?

... 中文怎么说？

... Zhōngwén zěnme shuō?

Could you find someone who can speak English?

能找个会说英文的人来吗？

Néngzhǎo gè huìshuō yīngwén de rén lái ma?

Can you understand when I speak Chinese?

你能听懂我的中文吗？

Nǐ néng tīng dǒng wǒ de zhōngwén ma?

I'm a tourist

我来旅游

Wǒ lái lǚyóu

I've come to teach English

我是来教英文的

Wǒ shì lái jiāo yīngwén de

I've come on a package tour

我是随旅游团来的

Wǒ shì súi lǚyóu tuán lái de

I'm here on business

我是来做生意的

Wǒ shì lái zuò shēngyì de

What should I call you?

我怎么称呼你呢？

Wǒ zěnme chēnghū nǐ ne?

Sorry I can't remember your name

对不起, 我记不起你的名字了

Dùi bù qǐ, wǒ jì bù qǐ nǐde míngzi le

Thank you for your help

谢谢你帮忙

Xièxie nǐ bāngmáng

Grammar

- Chinese grammar is a lot simpler than the grammar of many European languages, and it is well worth learning the following rules.

Word Order

- Chinese word order is much the same as in English, ie subject–verb–object.

Wǒ shì Yīngguó ren
I am English man

Wǒ bù dǒng Zhōngwén
I don't understand Chinese

Nouns and Pronouns

- There is no word for 'the' in Chinese. Where you would say 'I see the dog' in English, in Chinese you would say 'I see dog'.
- Chinese nouns do not have plural forms, ie they do not add 'e' or 'es' as in English. The plural is normally shown by the 'classifier' (see below).
- Subject and object pronouns are the same in Chinese, ie *wǒ* can mean 'I' or 'me', and *tā* can mean 'he', 'she', 'him' or 'her'.
- To make these plural, *men* is added, so *wǒmen* can mean 'we' or 'us', and *tāmen* can mean 'they' or 'them'.
- The word *de* is used to form possessives:
  wǒ = I, *wǒ de* = my/mine
  nǐ = you, *nǐ de* = your/yours
  Běijīng de = Beijing's
- *De* can also be used to form adjectives from nouns:
  měi = beauty, *měi de* = beautiful
  xiāng = sweetness, *xiāng de* = sweet
  cháng = length, *cháng de* = long

Classifiers (or measure words)

- These words are most commonly used in English when talking about food and drink: in the phrase 'a bottle of wine', bottle is the classifier, ie it tells you how much wine we are talking about. These words are used much more in Chinese, so where a phrase like 'two books' has no classifier in English, it does in Chinese: *liǎng běn shū*. There are many different classifiers in Chinese, but if you are not sure which one to use, say *gè*, which is a general word and will be understood in most situations.

● The number or quantity of Chinese nouns is expressed not by a change in the noun itself but by the use of different quantifying expressions before the noun:

three people	三个人
	sān ge rén
four books	四本书
	sì běn shū
ten knives	十把刀
	shí bǎ dāo

Verbs

● Chinese verbs are much simpler than English verbs: they do not change their form according to the subject, nor do they change from singular to plural. There is also only one form of the present tense, so *wǒ lái* can mean 'I come' or 'I am coming', *nǐ lái* can mean 'you come' or 'you are coming', *tā lái* can mean 'he/she comes' or 'he/she is coming' and so on.

● To form past tenses, the words *guò* or *le* are added to the present tense form to show that the action has been completed.

Tā chī fàn le
She/he (has) had a meal

Wǒmen qù guò Běijīng
We went/have been to Beijing

● The future tense is the same as the present tense, but with an added phrase to show that the action has not yet taken place.

Wǒ míngtiān qù Zhōngguó
I tomorrow go China = I will go to China tomorrow

● Where it is not possible to add a phrase like 'tomorrow' to show the future, you can use the word *yào*:

Wǒ yào qù Zhōngguó =I will go to China

● The word *yào* can also be used to express a desire:

Wǒ yào hē kāfēi
I want to drink coffee

Questions

● To form a question, you simply add the word *ma* on to the end of a statement:

Nín jiǎng Yīngwén ma?
You speak English = Do you speak English?

● Another useful way of forming questions is to use *yǒu* (there is/are) and its opposite *méi yǒu* (there isn't/aren't):

Fángjiān lǐ yǒu rèshuǐ ma?
room in there is hot water = Is there hot water in the room?

Fángjiān lǐ méi yǒu rèshuǐ ma?
room in there isn't hot water = Isn't there any hot water in the room?

● Unlike English, Chinese question words do not change the word order in the sentence:

Zhè shì shénme?	= (literally) This is what?
	= What is this?
Nín bù xǐhuān Běijīng ma?	= (literally) You not like Beijing?
	= Don't you like Beijing?

Negatives

● The word *bú* is used before a verb to make it negative in the present tense.

You are Smith Mr = Are you Mr Smith?	I not am = No, I'm not
Nǐ shì Shǐmìsī xiāngsheng ma?	*Wǒ bú shì*

Grammar

- *Méiyŏu* is used to make *yŏu* (to have) negative, and is also used in the past tenses.

Yŏu qiānzhèng ma?
Have visa = Do you
have a visa?

Wŏ méiyŏu qiānzhèng
I not have visa = No, I
don't have a visa

Wŏ méi yùdìng fángjiān
I not book(ed) room = I
haven't booked a room

Wŏ méi hē báijiŭ
I not drink Chinese
wine = I haven't drunk
Chinese wine

Yes and No

- There are no specific words in Chinese for yes or no. The best way to indicate these words is to repeat the verb from the question either positively or negatively as appropriate.

Nĭ shì Lĭ xiăojie ma? Are you Miss Li?	*Shì* Yes	*Bú shì* No
Nĭ hē báijiŭ ma? Do you drink wine	*Hē* Yes	*Bú he* No
Nĭ qù guò Bĕijīng ma? Have you been to Beijing?	*Qù guò* Yes	*Méi qùguò* No

Abbreviations

- You may find that many Chinese expressions are abbreviated, especially when they consist of several two-syllable words. Abbreviations are made by selecting key syllables and dropping the rest:

Beijing University	北京大学 *Bĕijīng Dàxue*
becomes	北大 *Bĕi-Dà*
underground	地下铁路 *Dìxiàtĭelù*
becomes	地铁 *Dì-Tĭe*

ARRIVAL AND DEPARTURE

- You need a visa to enter China which specifies the dates between which you may stay in China. If you wish to stay longer, do not forget to extend your visa officially, otherwise you will be fined.
- Some items, such as watches, cameras, radios, jewellery and tape recorders, should be declared on the form provided when you enter China and taken out of the country when you leave in order to avoid duty. You may be asked to produce these items upon departure by the customs officer, so any loss or theft of these should be reported immediately.
- Check the customs allowances when you enter China, as these tend to be fairly strict, especially concerning money. You are not permitted to take any Chinese currency into the country, and you must show your exchange receipts in order to change money on departure.

Customs

● There will almost certainly be someone who speaks English at the Customs post, but here are a few phrases just in case.

My surname is ...	我姓 *Wǒ xìng ...*
My name is ...	我的名字叫 *Wǒde míngzi jiào ...*
I'm from ...	我从 ... 来的 *Wǒ cóng ... lái de*
Britain	英国 *Yīngguó*
Ireland	爱尔兰 *Ài'ěrlán*
America	美国 *Měiguó*
Canada	加拿大 *Jiānádà*
Australia	澳大利亚 *Àodàlìyà*
New Zealand	新西兰 *Xīnxīlán*
Here is my passport	这是我的护照 *Zhè shì wǒde hùzhào*

You may hear:

你叫什么名字？ *Nǐ jiào shénme míngzi?*	What is your name?
你姓什么？ *Nǐ xìng shénme?*	What is your surname?
你从哪来？ *Nǐ cóng nǎr lái*	Where do you come from?
请拿护照看一下 *Qǐng ná hùzhào kán yí xià*	May I see your passport, please?

有签证吗？
Yǒu qiānzhèng ma?

Where is the visa?

请打开背包
Qǐng dǎkāi bēibāo

Please open your bag/case

你可以走了
Nín kéyǐ zǒule

You may go now

有健康证明书吗？
Yǒu jiànkāng zhèngmíng shūma?

Have you got your health certificate?

你的签证有问题
Nǐde qiānzhèng yǒu wèntí

There is something wrong with your visa

你有几件行李？
Nǐ yǒu jǐjiàn xíngli?

How many pieces of luggage do you have?

请把行李放这
Qǐng bǎ xíngli fàng zhè

Put your luggage here, please

这是你的行李吗？
Zhè shì nǐde xíngli ma?

Is this your luggage?

行李超重
Xíngli chāozhòng

You have excess luggage

这件不能免税
Zhèijiàn bùnéng miǎn shùi

This is not duty free

这件东西得留下
Zhèijiàn dōngxi děi liúxià

You'll have to leave it here

请跟我来
Qǐng gēn wǒ lái

Come with me, please

Luggage and Porters

● It is difficult to find porters at Chinese airports, and there are very few luggage trolleys. The best thing you can do is travel light. It is also wise to choose sturdy suitcases and bags, as Chinese luggage handlers are notoriously careless.

Where can I ...?

在哪里 ...？
Zài nǎli ...?

... claim my luggage

取行李

... qǔ xíngli

... check in my luggage

托运行李

... tuōyùn xíngli

Where can I find ...?

哪里有 ...?

Nǎli yǒu ...?

... a luggage trolley

手推车

... shǒu tuī chē

... a porter

行李员/搬运工

... xíngli yuán/bānyùn gōng

How much should I pay (for the excess luggage)?

我该交多少钱 (行李超重)?

Wǒ gāi jiāo duōshao qián (xíngli chāozhòng)?

My (bag/suitcase) is missing

我的 (包/手提袋) 不见了

Wǒde (bāo/shǒutídài) bú jiàn le

Asking directions

Where is the ...?

... 在哪里?

... zài nǎli?

... airport

机场 ...

Jīchǎng ...

... bus stop

汽车站 ...

Qìchē zhàn ...

... railway station

火车站 ...

Huǒchē zhàn ...

... public telephone

公用电话 ...

Gōngyòng diànhuà

... restaurant

餐馆 ...

Cānguǎn ...

... terminal

终点

Zhōngdiǎn ...

How do I get to ...?	去 ... 怎么走？ *Qù ... zěnme zǒu?*
... the Chinese International Travel Service	中国国际旅行社 *... Zhōngguó guójì lǚxíngshè ...*
... the hotel	旅社 *... lǚshè ...*
... this address	这个地址 *... zhèige dìzhǐ ...*

You may hear:

往 ... 走 *Wǎng ... zǒu*	**Go ...**
前 *... qián ...*	**... straight on**
北 *... běi ...*	**... north**
南 *... nán ...*	**... south**
东 *... dōng ...*	**... east**
西 *... xī ...*	**... west**
往（左/右）拐 *Wǎng (zuǒ/yòu) guǎi*	**Turn (left/right)**
过路口 *Guò lùkǒu*	**Cross the street**
到 ... 下车 *dào ... xiàchē*	**Get off at ...**
在 ... 前面 *zài ... qiánmiàn*	**in front of ...**

在 ... 后面 *zài ... hòumiàn*	behind ...
在 ... 左面 *zài ... zuǒmiàn*	to the left of ...
在 ... 右面 *zài ... yòumiàn*	to the right of ...

Taxis

- Taxi ranks can be found at hotels, stations, the main sights and other places frequented by tourists. If you cannot find a taxi, for example late at night, you can phone for one, stating location, your destination and the number of people in the party. You will find the number in the telephone directory under 出租车 *chūzū chē* (taxi). Most Chinese taxi drivers are honest and will charge you according to the mileage on the clock. You may want to check this yourself at the beginning and end of the journey to make sure.

Where is the taxi rank?	出租车在哪里？ *Chūzū chē zài nǎli?*
I want to go to (the airport/ the Friendship Hotel)	我要去(飞机场/友谊宾馆) *Wǒ yào qù (fēijīchǎng/yǒuyì bīnguǎn)*
How much will the fare be?	票价多少 *Piàojià duōshao?*
This is my baggage/suitcase	这是我的行李/手提包 *Zhèshì wǒde xíngli/shǒutí bāo*
Please drive a little (faster/more slowly)	请开(快/慢)点 *Qǐng kāi (kuài/màn) diǎn*
Is it far from the airport?	离机场远吗？ *Lí jīchǎng yuǎn ma?*
Do I pay according to mileage?	是计程车吗？ *Shì jìchéngchē ma?*

Departure

● When you leave China, you may be asked a few
questions when you clear customs.

You may hear:	
这是什么？ *Zhè shì shénme?*	**What is this?**
这些是什么？ *Zhèxiē shì shénme?*	**What are these?**
这些不许带出国 *Zhèxiē bùxǔ dài chūguó*	**You are not allowed to take this out of the country**
你身上有什么？ *Nǐ shēnshang yǒu shénme?*	**What have you got on you?**
请拿好 ... *Qǐng ná hǎo ...*	**Please take care of your ...**

I've got ...	我有 *Wǒ yǒu ...*
... cigarettes	烟 *... yān*
... wine	酒 *... jiǔ*
... medicine	药 *... yào*
... documents	文件 *... wénjiàn*
... video tapes	录相带 *... lùxiàng dài*
... cassetters	录音带 *... lùyīn dài*
... a bunch of keys	一串钥匙 *... yíchuàn yàoshi*

Arrival and Departure

Where do we check in?

在哪里托运行李？
Zài nǎli tuōyùn xíngli?

What time does our flight leave?

我们的航班几点起飞？
Wǒménde hángbān jǐdiǎn qǐfēi?

Here's my boarding card

这是我的登机牌
Zhèshì wǒde dēngjīpái

Can I take this on board?

我可以把这个带上飞机吗？
Wǒ kéyǐ bǎ zhège dàishang fēijī ma?

Is there a duty-free shop?

有免税商店吗？
Yǒu miǎnshuì shāngdiàn ma?

This is my hand luggage

这是我的手提行李
Zhèshì wǒde shǒutíxíngli

Can I change my flight?

我能换个行班吗？
Wǒ néng huàngè hángbān ma?

Is the flight on time?

飞机会准时吗？
Fēijī huì zhǔnshí ma?

Is the flight delayed?

飞机晚点了吗？
Fēijī wǎndiǎn le ma?

I've missed my plane

我没赶上飞机
Wǒ méi gǎnshang fēijī

ACCOMMODATION

- When referring to hotels, the most common Chinese words are 旅馆 *lǔguǎn,* 旅社 *lǔshè* and 旅店 *lǔdiàn.* 宾馆 *bīnguǎn* is a hotel for important or foreign guests in particular. Many large businesses have their own hostels for guests, called 招待所 *zhāodàisuǒ.* Some restaurants now offer an accommodation service as well. In terms of facilities, 宾馆 *bīnguǎn* are large and well-equipped, while 旅店 *lǔdiàn* are small, commonplace and, needless to say, cheap.
- Most tourist hotels in China were formerly high-class government guest houses or hotels. Rooms in these hotels are generally graded into luxury, first and second classes. Luxury rooms are two- or three-room suites, while first and second class have one room. Usually only luxury and first class rooms have *en suite* bathrooms.

- Most tourist hotels provide the following services: shops, hairdressers/barbers, bookshops, post and telecommunications offices, Bureau de Change, taxi services and restaurants. The latter usually cater for Chinese and western tastes, and will organise banquets and cocktail parties. See pages 22, 32, 33, 38, 100 and 113 for phrases.

- In some of the big hotels, buildings are named according to their geographical location. In the Friendship Hotel in Beijing, for instance, the different buildings are named Southeast Area (东南区 *Dōngnánqū*), Southwest Area (西南区 *Xīnánqū*). Points of the compass are also used in giving general directions, so you might be told 'Go straight on, then turn north and then east' if you asked for directions to your room. Use the following diagram to familiarise yourself with the compass points:

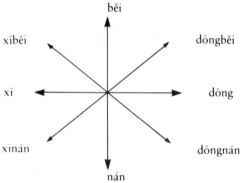

běi

xīběi   dōngběi

xī   dōng

xīnán   dōngnán

nán

- In China, men and women are housed in different sections unless they are married. Co-habitation of unmarried couples in hotels is considered inappropriate and therefore not allowed.

- If you have any problems or queries, ask your floor monitor 服务员 *fúwùyuán*.

Where is the hotel?	哪里有旅店？ *Nǎli yǒu lǚdiàn?*
Is it within walking distance?	走去可以吗？ *Zǒuqù kéyǐ ma?*

At the reception desk

Do you have any rooms free?	请问，有房间吗？ *Qǐngwèn, yǒu fángjiān ma?*
I'd like ...	我要 ... *Wǒ yào ...*
... a single room	单间 *... dānjiān*
... a double room	双人房间 *... shuāngrén fángjiān*
... a suite	套间 *... tàojiān*
I'd like a room with ...	我想要有 ... 的房间 *Wó xiǎng yào yǒu ... de fángjiān*
... a double bed	双人床 *... shuāng rén chuáng ...*
... a bath	洗澡间 *... xǐzǎojiān ...*
... shower	淋浴 *... línyù ...*
... balcony	阳台 *... yángtái ...*
How much is it per person per night?	一个人一晚上多少钱？ *Yíge rén yì wǎnshang duōshao qián?*
Have you got anything cheaper?	有更便宜点的房间吗？ *Yǒu gèng piányi diǎn de fángjiān ma?*
How much is it if we share?	我们合住要多少钱？ *Wǒmen hé zhù yào duōshao qián?*

Are meals included?	伙食在内吗？ *Huǒshí zài nèi ma?*
How many meals are included?	几顿饭？ *Jǐdùn fàn?*

● For information on taking meals in your hotel, see page 37.

You may hear:

什么样的房间？ *Shénme yàng de fángjiān?*	What kind of room would you like?
您定了房间了吗？ *Nín dìngle fángjiān le ma?*	Have you got a reservation?
二楼 *Èr lóu*	It's on the second floor
都有，但没有空调 *Dōuyǒu, dàn méiyǒu kōngtiáo*	It has everything except air conditioning
我们给你开门 *Wǒmen gěi nǐ kāimén*	We will unlock the door for you
您住几天？ *Nín zhù jǐtiān?*	How many days are you staying?
请先填表 *Qǐng xiān tiánbiǎo*	Please could you fill in the form
可以进来吗？ *Kéyǐ jìnlai ma?*	May I come in?
一人一天一百元 *Yìrén yìtiān yìbǎi yuán*	100 yuan per person per night
一天三顿饭 *Yìtiān sāndùn fàn*	Three meals a day
饭钱在内 *Fànqián zài nèi*	Meals are included
没有便宜的了 *Méiyǒu piányi de le*	Sorry, we haven't anything cheaper
十二点前结帐 *Shíèr diǎn qián jiézhàng*	Please pay the bill before noon

Accommodation

I have a reservation	我已经预订了房间 *Wǒ yǐjīng yùdìng le fángjiān*
Here is my name. Could you look for it, please?	这是我的名字, 请查一下 *Zhè shì wǒde míngzi, qǐng chá yíxià*
Which floor is my room on?	我的房间在几楼？ *Wǒde fángjiān zài jǐlóu?*
What number is it?	多少号 *Duōshao hào?*

Is there ...?	房间里有 ... 吗？ *fángjiān lǐ yǒu ... ma?*

... heating	暖气 *... nuǎnqì ...*
... air conditioning	空调 *... kōngtiáo ...*
... hot water	热水 *... rèshuǐ ...*
... television	电视 *... diànshì ...*
... telephone	电话 *... diànhuà ...*

Shall I keep the room key?	我自己带钥匙吗？ *Wǒ zìjǐ dài yàoshi ma?*
Could you wake me at 6.30 am, please floor monitor?	服务员, 早晨六点半叫醒我 *Fúwùyuán, zǎochén liùdiǎn bàn jiàoxǐng wǒ*
Come in, please	请进 *Qǐngjìn*

Complaints

Can I see the manager?	我可以见经理吗？ *Wǒ kéyǐ jiàn jīnglǐ ma?*
The bulb in my room has blown	我的灯泡坏了 *Wǒde dēngpào huài le*

| My room has no ... | 我的房间没有 ... 了 |
| | *Wǒde fángjiān méiyǒu ... le* |

| ... hot water | 热水 |
| | *... rèshuǐ ...* |

| ... electricity | 电 |
| | *... diàn ...* |

| ... toilet paper | 卫生纸 |
| | *... wèishēngzhǐ ...* |

| ... tea | 茶叶 |
| | *... cháyè ...* |

| My toilet is blocked | 我的厕所堵了 |
| | *Wǒde cèsuǒ dǔ le* |

| My window is jammed | 我的窗户卡住了 |
| | *Wǒde chuānghu kǎ zhù le* |

| The socket doesn't work | 插座不好使 |
| | *Chāzuò bù hǎo shǐ* |

| The sink is blocked | 水池堵了 |
| | *Shuǐchí dǔ le* |

| The people next door are too noisy | 我隔壁的人太吵 |
| | *Wǒ gébì de rén tài chǎo* |

| My room is very (hot/cold) | 我的房间太 (热/冷) 了 |
| | *Wǒde fángjiān tài (rè/lěng) le* |

| Is there a dry-cleaning service? | 有干洗店吗？ |
| | *Yǒu gānxǐ diàn ma?* |

| I need another (blanket/pillow) | 我还需要 (一条毯子/一个枕头) |
| | *Wǒ hái xūyào (yìtiáo tǎnzi/yīgè zhěntou)* |

| Where is the laundry? | 洗衣房在哪里？ |
| | *Xǐyīfáng zài nǎli?* |

| Can I get my laundry back tomorrow? | 我明天可以取衣服吗？ |
| | *Wǒ míngtiān kéyǐ qǔ yīfu ma?* |

| Please do not disturb | 我睡觉时不要打搅我 |
| | *Wǒ shuìjiào shí búyào dǎjiao wǒ* |

Telephoning from the hotel

Can I make an international call here?
我能在这打个国际电话吗？
Wǒ néng zàizhè dǎ ge guójì diànhuà ma?

Can I dial direct?
是直拨电话吗？
Shì zhíbō diànhuà ma?

My (country code/city code) is ...
我的 (国家代号/城市代号) 是 ...
Wǒ de (guójiā dàihào/ chéngshì dàihào) shì ...

Can I dial from my room?
我可以在我房间里打吗？
Wǒ kěyǐ zài wǒ fángjiānli dǎ ma?

Do I have to pay a deposit?
要交押金吗？
Yào jiāo yājīn ma?

Shall I wait here or in my room?
是在这等呢还是在我房间等呢？
Shì zài zhè děng ne háishì zài wǒ fángjiān děng ne?

How long does it take?
要多久呢？
Yào duō jiǔ ne?

Do I have to pay the phone bill today?
今天要付电话费吗？
Jīntiān yào fù diànhuàfèi ma?

● For other telephoning phrases, see page 116.

At the barber's

barber's (shop)
理发店 (馆)
lǐfàdiàn (guǎn)

barber
理发师
lǐfàshī

beauty parlour
美容店
měiróng diàn

Can I have my hair cut here?
我能在这理发吗？
Wǒ néng zài zhè lǐfà ma?

Is there a hairdressing salon?
有美发厅吗？
Yǒu měifà tīng ma?

I'd like my hair (permed/dyed)
我想 (烫/染) 头发
Wǒ xiǎng (tàng/rǎn) tóufa

31

Checking out

We are leaving (today/tomorrow)	我们(今天/明天)走 *Wǒmén (jīntiān/míngtiān) zǒu*
I'd like to pay the bill	我要付帐 *Wǒ yào fùzhàng*
At 9 am	上午九点 *Shàng wǔ jiúdiǎn*
Do you accept (credit cards/cheques)?	你收(信用卡/支票)吗？ *Nǐ shōu (xìnyòngkǎ/zhīpiào) ma?*
Shall I hand the keys in now?	现在就交钥匙吗？ *Xiànzài jiù jiāo yàoshi ma?*
Can I pay in (RMB/FEC)?	我可以付(人民币/外汇卷)吗？ *Wǒ kéyǐ fù (Rénmínbì/ Wàihùijuàn) ma?*
Can I have my deposit back?	能还给我押金吗？ *Néng huán gěi wǒ yājīn ma?*
Would it be possible to leave my baggage here for a few hours?	可以把行李放这里几小时吗？ *Kéyǐ bǎ xínglǐ fàng zhèli jǐ xiǎo shí ma?*
I've enjoyed my stay here very much	我在这里过得很愉快 *Wǒ zài zhèli guò de hěn yúkuài*
Thank you very much for all your help	非常感谢你的帮助 *Fēicháng gǎnxiē nǐ de bāngzhù*

- Generally speaking, it is assumed that you will be staying in hotels in China. Accommodation such as youth hostels, self-catering, staying with a family or even campsites is not usually available to foreign tourists, although it may be worth checking with a specialist travel agency.
- Costs vary according to the class of hotel and the season. High season is usually from June until September.

EATING OUT

- China is, of course, famous for its cuisine, thanks to the ubiquitous Chinese restaurant. In China itself, the choice is even more varied, but Chinese cooking has four main schools, each with its own special features.
- *Northern Chinese cuisine*, also called Mandarin cuisine, comes from the northern provinces. Wheat products form the basis of many of their dishes which tend to be slightly salty, sweet and sometimes spicy. The most famous of these is Peking roast duck.
- *Western Chinese cooking* comes from the Sichuan and Hunan Provinces, where hot pepper is used a lot. You will see many dishes covered with red chilli powder.
- *Eastern Chinese cooking*, from around the Shanghai region, features seafood and fresh vegetables, especially bamboo shoots. It is often flavoured with soy sauce and sugar.

- *Southern Chinese cuisine*, also known as Cantonese, is the kind usually found in western Chinese restaurants, and has its roots in Guangdong, Fujian and Taiwan regions. Some Chinese consider their dishes to be bland and 'foreign' tasting, as they do not use strong seasonings and some include foreign ingredients.

Where can I find a ...?	哪里有 ... ? *Nǎli yǒu ...?*
... western restaurant	西餐馆 ... *xīcān guǎn*
... Chinese restaurant	中餐馆 ... *zhōngcān guǎn*
... Shanghai restaurant	上海餐馆 ... *shànghǎi cānguǎn*
... Sichuan restaurant	四川餐馆 ... *sìchuān cānguǎn*
... Cantonese restaurant	广东餐馆 ... *guǎngdōng cānguǎn*
... Mandarin restaurant	北方餐馆 ... *běifāng cānguǎn*
... Moslem restaurant	清真馆 ... *qīngzhēn guǎn*
Is there a western dining room here?	有西餐厅吗 ? *Yǒu xīcān tīng ma?*

At a restaurant

- Many big restaurants in China have separate sections where foreign guests are served. The service there is better, the facilities cleaner, and the prices are, of course, higher. You can have meals with the Chinese if you want, but this will often mean putting up with slower service, a lot of noise and bustle and not such hygienic surroundings. If this appeals to you, look for a 饭店 *fàndiàn*, which, in addition to providing a taste of the 'real' China, will usually be open early in the morning and late in the evening. Look for the sign 营业时间 *Yíngyè shíjiān* to find the opening hours.

● If you are planning to go out to eat in a group, it is wise to reserve a table in advance. You can ask your guide or another Chinese person to do this if you do not feel confident about speaking on the phone. In addition to the usual details (ie how many people are coming, what time you want the table), they will often want to know your nationality, the amount you intend to spend and the number of dishes you are likely to order.

Is there a restaurant nearby?	这里有饭店吗？ *Zhèli yǒu fàndiàn ma?*
Waiter, we'd like three dishes	师傅，我们要三个菜 *Shīfu, wǒmen yào sānge cài*
I eat vegetables, but not meat	我吃素菜，不吃肉 *Wǒ chī sùcài, bù chī ròu*

I'd like ...	我想要 *Wó xiǎng yào ...*
... rice	米饭 *... mǐfàn*
... noodles	面条 *... miàntiáo*
... bread	面包 *... miànbāo*
... pancake	饼 *... bǐng*

● For other dishes, see page 41.

I don't drink wine	我不喝酒 *Wǒ bù hē jiǔ*

This dish is too ...	这个菜太 *Zhèige cài tài ...*

... oily	油腻 *... yóunì*
... salty	咸 *... xián*
... hot	辣 *... là*
... cold	凉 *... liáng*

I've had enough	够了 *Gòule*
Waiter/waitress the bill, please	服务员，请算帐 *Fúwùyuán, qǐng suànzhàng*
Where should we pay?	到哪里付款？ *Dào nǎli fùkuǎn?*

You may hear:

您吃 ... 吗？ *Nín chī ... ma?*	**Do you eat ...?**
肉 *... ròu ...*	... meat
海物 *... hǎiwù ...*	... seafood
素菜 *... sùcài ...*	... vegetables
鸡 *... jī ...*	... chicken
鱼 *... yú ...*	... fish
鸡蛋 *... jīdàn ...*	... eggs

主食要什么？	What do you want with
Zhǔshí yào shénme?	your meal? (eg rice, noodles)

要汤吗？	Would you like any soup?
Yào tāng ma?	

你们要什么酒？	Would you like any wine?
Nǐmen yào shénme jiǔ?	

您用筷子吗？	Can you use chopsticks?
Nín yòng kuàizi ma?	

您还要点什么？	Would you like anything
Nín hài yào diǎn shénme?	else?

In the hotel

Foreign visitors usually have their meals in the dining room of the hotel they are staying in. The three meals of the day are: 早饭 *zǎofàn* (breakfast), 午饭 *wǔfàn* (lunch) and 晚饭 *wǎnfàn* (supper). There is usually a sign indicating meal times. Food can be prepared in both the western and Chinese ways, and parties of any size can usually be catered for.

I'd like western breakfast	早饭要西餐
	Zǎofàn yào xīcān

I'd like to book a table for supper the day after tomorrow	后天我想预订一桌晚饭
	Hòutiān wó xiǎng yùdìng yìzhuō wǎnfàn

How much will it cost?	一桌要多少钱？
	Yìzhuō yào duōshao qián?

Two bottles of beer	两瓶啤酒
	Liǎngpíng píjiǔ

One bottle of Chinese wine	一瓶白酒
	Yìpíng báijiǔ

Can we pay separately?	我们可以分别付款吗？
	Wǒmen kéyǐ fénbié fùkuǎn ma?

37

You may hear:

您明天三顿饭都在这吃吗？
Nín míngtiān sāndùn fàn dōu zài zhè chī ma?

Will you have all three meals tomorrow?

午饭要有酒吗？
Wǔfàn yào yǒu jiǔ ma?

Would you like some wine with your lunch?

喝白酒还是啤酒？
Hē báijiǔ, háishì píjiǔ?

Would you like Chinese wine or beer?

还要什么？
Hái yào shénme?

Would you like anything else?

多少人？
Duōshao rén?

How many of you are there?

多少个菜？
Duōshao ge cài?

How many dishes will you want?

酒水不在内
Jiǔshuǐ búzài nèi

Wine and drink are not included

At a formal meal or banquet

- If you are lucky enough to be invited to one of these occasions (and it is more likely that you might think, as the Chinese love to entertain foreigners in this way) here are some guidelines to help you.
- Firstly, build up an appetite before you go – there are often more than ten dishes, and your plate will be filled by your host if you empty it, so pace yourself for each dish. You should always try at least a mouthful of each dish, even if you don't like it or have had enough.
- The meal will generally start with a few cold platters such as Chinese salad (*liángcài*), chopped marinated beef, peanuts, preserved eggs and so on. Then comes the main course, which is a series of hot dishes served one after the other. These are usually designed to complement each other in colour, flavour and taste, so there will be a variety of salty, sweet, sour and

spicy dishes. A big bowl of soup or a large fish on a platter indicates that the main course is coming to an end. It will be followed by rice, noodles or some other wheaten food.

- Desserts are not common in China, and cheese is virtually unheard of. The meal will usually end with some fruit, of which China has a vast selection. The Chinese like to see their guests eat and drink well, and will make sure your plate and glass are kept full. It is up to you to say that you have had enough – it is not considered impolite to do so.

- Chinese wines are stronger than whisky, so be careful how much you drink. The Chinese consider it undignified to get drunk in front of strangers and will not do so themselves. It is customary not to drink until the host has proposed the first toast, and when you have finished your drink, you turn your glass upside down to show that you have drained it. Do not, however, feel pressurised into drinking – it is perfectly acceptable to ask for fruit juice, tea or mineral water.

Cheers!	干杯 *Gānbēi*
I would like to propose a toast ...	现在, 我提议 ... 干杯！ *Xiànzài, wǒ tíyì ... gānbēi*
... to your health	为你们的健康 *... wèi nǐmen de jiànkāng ...*
... to the health of our host	为主人的健康 *... wèi zhǔrén de jiànkāng ...*
Please could you get me ...	请再拿 *Qǐng zài ná ...*
... a pair of chopsticks	一双筷子 *... yìshuāng kuàizi*
... a knife	一把刀 *... yī bǎ dāo*
... a fork	一个叉子 *... yíge chāzi*

Eating Out

... a cup
一个杯子
... yíge bēizi

... a spoon
一把匙子
... yìbǎ chízi

... a few napkins
几张餐巾
... jǐzhāng cānjīn

... some toothpicks
一些牙签儿
... yìxiē yáqiānr

I like Chinese food
喜欢中国饭
Xǐhuān zhōngguó fàn

I have had enough, thank you
吃好了，谢谢
Chīhǎo le, xièxie

I don't eat/like ...
我不吃
Wǒ bù chī ...

I can't drink anymore
不能再喝了
Bùnéng zài hē le

I'm sorry, I've had a bit too much to drink
请原谅，我真的
Qǐng yuánliàng, wǒ zhēn de bùxíng le

You may hear:

请坐
Qǐng zuò
Please take a seat

请 (吃菜/喝酒)
Qǐng (chīcài/hējiǔ)
Please help yourself to (food/drink)

喜欢中国饭吗？
Xǐhuan zhōngguó fàn ma?
Do you like Chinese food?

您吃好了吗？
Nín chīhǎo le ma?
Have you had enough?

喜欢吃 ... 吗？
Xǐhuan chī ... ma?
Do you like ...?

您再吃点吧
Ní zài chī diǎn ba
Have a bit more

Thank you for your
hospitality

感谢您的盛情款待
*Gǎnxiè nín de shèngqíng
kuǎndài*

Where can I wash my hands?

哪里可以洗手？
Nǎli kéyi xíshǒu?

On the menu

Cold dishes/hors d'oeuvres

冷盘 *lěngpán*	cold dish
酱牛肉 *jiàng niúròu*	marinated beef
花生米 *huāshēngmǐ*	peanuts
凉菜 *liángcài*	Chinese salad
松花蛋 *sōnghuā dàn*	preserved eggs/thousand-year eggs
螃蟹 *pángxiè*	crab
海蜇皮 *hǎizhépí*	jelly fish
榨菜 *zhàcài*	Sichuan preserved vegetables/hot pickled mustard root
烤鸭 *kǎoyā*	roast duck
烧鸡 *shāojī*	roast chicken
香肠 *xiāngcháng*	sausage
凉粉 *liángfěn*	bean jelly
粉丝 *fěnsī*	vermicelli (made from wheat starch)

41

Eating Out

青椒 qīngjiāo	green pepper	胡萝卜 húluóbo	carrot
生菜 shēngcài	lettuce	肉丝 ròusī	shredded meat
菠菜 bōcài	spinach	虾仁儿 xiārénr	shrimp meat
西红柿 xīhóngshì	tomato	鸡蛋 jīdàn	egg

Hot dishes

热菜 rècài	hot dish
拔丝（苹果/香蕉/地瓜） básī (píngguǒ/xiāngjiāo/dìguā)	toffee (apples/bananas/sweet potatoes)
红烧（猪肉/牛肉/鱼/海参/茄子） hóngshāo (zhūròu/niúròu/yú/hǎishen/qiézi)	braised (pork/beef/fish/sea cucumber/aubergine)
糖醋排骨 tángcù páigǔ	sweet and sour spare ribs
木犀肉/木须肉 mùxīròu/mùxūròu	stir-fried pork with scrambled egg and black mushrooms
宫保（肉丁/鸡丁） gōngbào (ròudīng/jīdīng)	diced (pork/chicken) with hot pepper
涮羊肉 shuàn yángròu	Mongolian hot-pot (slices of lamb and assorted vegetables boiled and then dipped in a sauce)
葱爆羊肉 cōngbào yángròu	flash-fried lamb with spring onions
麻婆豆腐 mápó dòufu	bean curd with minced pork in a hot sauce
沙锅豆腐 shāguo dòufu	bean curd in casserole
炒（竹笋/豆芽） chǎo (zhúsǔn/dòuyár)	stir-fried (bamboo shoots/bean sprouts)

芹菜 qíncài	celery	豌豆 wāndòu	pea
白菜 báicài	Chinese leaves	芥蓝 gàilán	Chinese broccoli
蘑菇 mógu	mushroom	莲藕 lián'ǒu	lotus root
洋葱 yángcōng	onion	菜花 càihuā	cauliflower
菜豆 càidòu	French beans		

Seafood

对虾 duìxiā	prawn	蛤蜊 gélí	clam
龙虾 lóngxiā	lobster	鱿鱼 yóuyú	squid
蠔/蚝 háo	oyster	墨鱼 mòyú	cuttlefish

Soup

鸡蛋汤 jīdàn tāng	egg-drop soup
酸辣汤 suānlà tāng	hot sour soup
鱼翅汤 yúchì tāng	shark's fin soup
榨菜肉丝汤 zhàcài ròusī tāng	shredded pork and Sichuan preserved vegetable soup
火腿冬瓜汤 huótuǐ dōngguā tāng	ham and winter melon soup
排骨海带汤 páigǔ hǎidài tāng	spare rib and kelp soup
肉丸汤 ròuwán tāng	meatball soup
银耳汤 yín'ěr tāng	white fungi soup

Basics

米饭 mǐfàn	plain rice
炒饭 chǎofàn	fried rice
稀饭 xīfàn	porridge (made with rice)
八宝饭 bābǎo fàn	eight-treasure rice pudding
馒头 mántou	steamed bread
包子 bāozi	steamed, stuffed meat buns
豆沙包 dòushābāo	sweet bean buns
花卷儿 huājuǎnr	steamed, twisted rolls
锅贴儿 guōtiēr	pan-fried pork dumplings
饼 bǐng	Chinese pancake
春饼/薄饼 chūnbǐng/bóbǐng	Mandarin pancake (very thin)
烧麦 shāomài	open-topped steamed pork dumplings
春卷 chūnjuǎn	spring roll
油条 yóutiáo	cruller (a ring-shaped cake, deep-fat fried)
饺子 jiǎozi	meat dumplings
馄饨 húntun	wonton (a dumpling filled with spiced, minced pork served in soup)

面条 *miàntiáo*	noodles
炒面 *chǎomiàn*	fried noodles
担担面 *dāndānmiàn*	Sichuan spicy sesame noodles
烤面包 *kǎo miànbāo*	toast

Seasonings and sauces

胡椒 *hújiāo*	pepper
花椒 *huājiāo*	Chinese prickly ash
大料 *dàliào*	aniseed
盐 *yán*	salt
糖 *táng*	sugar
葱 *cōng*	leek/spring onion
蒜 *suàn*	garlic
酱油 *jiàngyóu*	soy sauce
醋 *cù*	vinegar
芝麻酱 *zhīmajiàng*	sesame paste
香油/麻油 *xiāngyóu/máyóu*	sesame oil
辣椒酱 *làjiāojiàng*	hot pepper sauce

蕃茄酱 *fānqiéjiàng*	tomato sauce/ketchup
味精 *wèijīng*	monosodium glutamate
姜 *jiāng*	ginger

Fruit

● Fruit is usually served as a dessert, but you can ask for it at any point during the meal.

May I have some ...		给我拿些 ... 行吗？ *Gěi wǒ ná xiè ... xíng ma?*	
... apples	苹果 ... *píngguǒ*	... cherries	樱桃 ... *yīngtao*
... bananas	香蕉 ... *xiāngjiāo*	... plums	李子 ... *lǐzi*
... pineapple	菠萝 ... *bōluó*	... apricots	杏 ... *xìng*
... oranges	桔子 ... *júzi*	... watermelon	西瓜 ... *xīguā*
... grapes	葡萄 ... *pútao*	... pears	梨 ... *lí*
... peaches	桃子 ... *táozi*	... jujubes (Chinese dates)	枣子 ... *zǎozi*
... lychee	荔枝 ... *lizhī*		

Beverages

白酒 *báijiǔ*	Chinese wine
葡萄酒 *pútao jiǔ*	wine
啤酒 *píjiǔ*	beer

汽水 *qìshuǐ*	soda/fizzy drink
矿泉水 *kuàngquán shuǐ*	mineral water
果汁 *guǒzhī*	fruit juice
威士忌 *wēishìjì*	whisky
白兰地 *báilándì*	brandy
香槟 *xiāngbīn*	champagne
牛奶 *niúnǎi*	milk
咖啡 *kāfēi*	coffee
茶 *chá*	tea
绿茶 *lǜchá*	green tea
红茶 *hóngchá*	black tea
茉莉花茶 *mòlihuā chá*	jasmine tea
酸奶 *suānnǎi*	yoghurt
豆浆 *dòujiāng*	soy milk
热可可 *rèkěke*	hot chocolate

- Most Chinese will understand western prounciation of spirits such as whisky and brandy. Alcohol is not generally drunk at meals, except for wine and certain strong spirits used for toasts. Beers are very much like their western counterparts.

- *Báijiǔ* literally means white wine and refers to the strong Chinese wine made from rice or grain, which is actually transparent, not white. Wine made from grapes or other fruit is *pútao* or *guójiǔ*. The strength of the wine should be shown on the label, ranging from the strongest (60°) to about 18°. To drink 60° *báijiǔ*, people use small handleless cups which double as measuring cups, so that you can see how much you've drunk. Be wary of Chinese wine at this strength, and remember that the groups of Chinese knocking it back in restaurants (sometimes as part of a drinking game) have had a lot of practice!

- If you don't want to drink alcohol, you can ask for a fruit juice, a soft drink or a mineral water. For example to ask for (a coke), you can say 有 (可口可乐) 吗？*yǒu (kékǒu kělè) ma?*

- Tea is drunk at any time of the day, and is taken without sugar or milk. The most popular varieties are black (fermented) tea, green tea and tea scented with jasmine or other flowers. Different regions have different ways of serving tea.

Breakfast

果酱 guǒjiàng	jam	肉松/鱼松 ròusōng/yúsōng	dried minced meat/fish
黄油 huángyóu	butter	蛋糕 dàngāo	cake
奶油 nǎiyóu	cream	糖 táng	sugar
蜂蜜 fēngmì	honey	两片烤面包 liǎngpiàn kǎo miànbào	two slices of toast
泡菜/咸菜 pàocài/xiáncài	pickled vegetable	煎鸡蛋 jiān jīdàn	fried eggs

- You will probably find both western and Chinese breakfasts served in your hotel. A Chinese breakfast might consist of steamed bread, jasmine tea, cakes, dried minced meat or fish, a sort of doughnut, soy milk and a rice and bean curd pudding.

ENTERTAINMENT
AND SPORT

- There is so much to see and do in China: opera, cinema, theatre, martial arts demonstrations, acrobatics plus many places of cultural and historical interest to visit. However, those hoping for an exciting nightlife will probably be disappointed as the little that is a available is usually difficult to find and often barred to foreigners if you do find it. Early to bed, early to rise is still the motto of many Chinese people.
- The best way of ensuring that you make the most of your stay in China is to follow the advice of your guide or host, and to take advantage of any organised entertainment.

One or two points that you should be aware of:

- Official Chinese policy forbids tipping, and most Chinese will refuse any tips offered. It is best to avoid this altogether, as it could cause embarassment.

49

● Some occasions, however, do call for some exchange of gifts. This is especially true when on official visits to , say, a school or factory. You will often be given a souvenir of your visit, and are expected to leave one in return. This exchange of tokens also takes place when someone invites you to dinner. In this case, a bunch of flowers is usually adequate, although most Chinese would prefer a more personal gift, perhaps a souvenir from home.

● When on tours or guided visits, make sure that you do not become separated from the rest of your party. This is often easily done, as many Chinese will stop westerners in order to try out their English or simply out of curiousity.

I'd like to see ...	我想看 *Wó xiǎng kàn ...*
... a film	电影 ... *diànyǐng*
... a play	话剧 ... *huàjù*
... a ballet	芭蕾舞 ... *bāléiwǔ*
... the Peking Opera	京剧 ... *jīngjù*
... a local opera	地方戏 ... *dìfāngxì*
... an acrobatics show	杂技表演 ... *zájì biáoyǎn*
... a martial arts demonstration	武术表演 ... *wǔshù biáoyǎn*
... a magic show	魔术 ... *móshù*
... a table tennis match	乒乓球 ... *pīngpōng qiú*

... a basketball match	篮球 ... *lánqiú*
... a football match	足球 ... *zúqiú*
... a volleyball match	排球 ... *páiqiú*
... a tennis match	网球 ... *wǎngqiú*
I'd like to go to ...	我想听 *Wó xiǎng tīng ...*
... a concert	音乐会 ... *yīnyuèhuì*
... a Chinese classical music concert	民乐演奏 ... *mínyuè yǎnzòu*

● Note that *kàn* is used when you are going to watch something and *tīng* when you are going to listen.

Cinema

Is there a ...?	演 ... 吗？ *Yǎn ... ma?*
... Chinese film	中国片 ... *zhōngguó piān ...*
... foreign film	外国片 ... *wàiguó piān ...*
... English film	英国片 ... *yīngguó piān ...*
... American film	美国片 ... *měiguó piān ...*
... martial arts/kungfu film	武术/武打片 ... *wǔshù/wúdǎ piān ...*

... thriller	惊险片 *... jīngxiǎn piān ...*
... documentary	记录片 *... jìlù piān ...*

Are there English subtitles?	有英文字幕吗？ *Yǒu yīngwén zìmù ma?*
Has the film been dubbed?	是翻译片吗？ *Shì fānyì piān ma?*

Tickets and performances

● Booking tickets is not normally something you will have to do, as it is usually taken care of by the travel agency or host organisation.

What time shall we meet?	几点集合？ *Jídiǎn jíhé?*
Where shall we meet?	在哪儿？ *Zàinǎr?*
What time is the (first/last) performance?	(第/最后)一场是什么时候？ *(Dì/zuìhòu) yìchǎng shì shénme shíhou?*
How much is it for an adult?	大人票一张多少钱？ *Dàrén piào yìzhāng duōshao qián?*
And for a child?	儿童票呢？ *Értóngpiào ne?*
I'd like tickets for two adults and one child	两张大人票，一张儿童票 *Liǎngzhāng dàrén piào, yìzhāng értóng piào*
I'd like a seat in the (circle/stalls)	我要(楼上/楼下)的座位 *Wǒyào (lóushàng/lóuxià) de zuòwèi*
I'd like a seat in the (front/back) row	我要(前排/后排)的座位 *Wǒ yào (qiánpái/hòupái) de zuòwèi*

Are there no tickets left?

票都售完了吗？
Piào dōu shòu wán le ma?

Who's playing the main part?

主演是谁？
Zhúyǎn shìshéi?

Is he/she famous?

他/她有名吗？
Tā yǒu míng ma?

Is there an usher?

有引座员吗？
Yǒu yǐn zuòyuán ma?

May I have a programme?

要一张节目单行吗？
Yào yìzhāng jiémùdān xíngma?

How long does the play last?

剧演多长时间？
Jù yǎn duōcháng shíjiān?

Is there an interval?

中间休息吗？
Zhōngjiān xiūxi ma?

What time does ... begin?

... 几点开始？
... jídiǎn kāishǐ?

What's on?

什么节目？
Shénme jiému?

You may hear:

今天我们看 ... *Jīntiān wǒmen kàn ...*	We'll go to ... today
马戏 ... *mǎxì*	... a circus
民间舞蹈 ... *mínjiān wúdǎo*	... some folk dancing
儿童歌舞 ... *értóng gēwǔ*	... a children's show
时装表演 ... *shízhuāng biáoyǎn*	... a fashion show
迪斯科 ... *dísīkē*	... a disco

Local opera

- As a country of ancient culture, China has a rich variety of stage arts, of which opera is the main form. There are over 360 different local operas, each province and autonomous region having its own opera. There are more than 3000 opera companies in the country, boasting over 200,000 professional artists. Beijing Opera, Shaoxing Opera and Henan Opera are popular throughout the nation, with the Beijing Opera as the most popular. It is China's leading opera company and combines opera-singing, music, dance and acrobatics into an impressive spectacle.

Dancing

- China has a long history of singing and dancing. Most of the 50 nationalities of the country are good at both. *Yangge*, a folk group dance depicting farming, is among the most beautiful dances of the Han nation. The *Andai* dance of the Mongols (Mongolians) with strong, rhythmic movements, the grape-picking dance of the Uygurs in Xinjiang with detailed description of the feelings, the *Guozhuang* dance of the Zangs (Tibetans), the reed-pipe dance of the Miaos with a great variety of action and the long-drum dance of the Koreans: all of them show their different national characteristics. The folk dances such as dragon dance, red-silk scarf dance and the flower-drum dance are popular among the countryfolk.
- Local discos are not usually open to foreigners, but you will probably find dancing of some kind at your hotel, where you will be welcome.
- Ballroom dancing is very popular, and you may be invited to a ball at a university or at a large company or factory.

Would you like to dance? 跳个舞好吗？
Tiào gè wǔ hǎo ma?

Yes, I'd love to 很高兴
Hěn gāoxìng

You are a good dancer	你的舞跳得很好 *Nǐ de wǔ tiào dě hénhǎo*
Thank you (for saying so)	谢谢夸奖 *Xièxie kuājiǎng*

Acrobatics

Acrobatics is another of the arts with a long history in China. Many parts of the performance, such as climbing the pole, are movements developed from hunting, fruit picking and other everyday activities of the past. Many of the props used in acrobatics, such as tables, chairs, ceramic jars and flower vases, are articles used in daily life. With these, the artists have created such items as 'bowls on head', 'plate-spinning' and 'hand-stands on piled chairs'. Diabolo or shuttlecock playing are refinements of popular Chinese sports and games.

Opinions

I really enjoyed the ... today	今天的 ... 真带劲 *Jīntiān de ... zhēn dàijìn*
The music is too loud	音乐太响了! *Yīnyuè tài xiǎng le*
I hate the loudspeaker on the train	我不喜欢火车上的广播 *Wǒ bù xǐhuān huǒchē shàngde guǎngbō*
It's a pity there is no English narration	没有英文解说太遗憾了 *Méiyǒu yīngwén jiěshuō tài yíhàn le*
I like Chinese ...	我喜欢中国 ... *Wǒ xǐhuān zhōngguó ...*
... acrobatics	杂技 *... zájì*
... opera	戏剧 *... xìjù*

Sport

● Exercise is an integral part of Chinese life, and
  the day often starts with some sort of communal
  work-out. If you go to parks and squares in China's
  major cities between 5am and 7am, you will see
  people doing their exercises, such as *Taiji* (a sort of
  traditional Chinese shadow boxing), *qigong* (a system
  of deep-breathing exercises), aerobics and jogging.

sports stadium	体育场 *tǐyùchǎng*
gymnasium	体育馆 *tǐyùguǎn*
swimming pool	游泳池 *yóuyǒng chí*
sports meeting	运动会 *yùndòng huì*
gymnastic display	体操表演 *tǐcāo biǎoyǎn*
ballgames	球赛 *qiúsài*
swimming and diving contest	游泳跳水比赛 *yóuyǒng tiàoshuǐ bǐsài*
marathon	马拉松赛 *mǎlāsōng sài*
athlete/sportsman/player	运动员 *yùndòng yuán*

Swimming and boating

● Swimming is very popular in China, and in warm
  weather the water is often so crowded that it is
  impossible to swim more than a couple of strokes.
  The Chinese prefer swimming in the sea, rivers or
  lakes, and consider swimming pools to be boring, so
  these may be less crowded.

- Temperature is not a governing factor when it comes to swimming. Some Chinese will swim quite happily in the winter months in sub-zero temperatures, even when they have to break the ice to do so. Seeing people in the water is not, therefore, a guarantee that the water is warm!
- There are no naturist beaches in China, and topless bathing is very rare. Take your cue from the people around you.

Can I swim here?	这里哪儿能游泳？ *Zhèli nǎr néng yóuyǒng?*
How much is admission?	门票多少钱？ *Ménpiào duōshao qián?*
Is it safe?	安全吗？ *Ānquán ma?*
Can I hire a boat?	租船可以吗？ *Zūchuán kéyǐ ma?*
There is a (lake/swimming pool)	有（湖/游泳池） *Yǒu (hú/yóuyǒng chí)*

Meeting People

- During the Cultural Revolution and for some years after, the Chinese were very reticent about making friends with foreigners, as this often led to them being suspected of spying. In recent years, however, things have changed, and the Chinese are a lot more eager to get to know foreigners visiting their country, although there are still some obvious cultural differences. There is much less physical contact between people, and couples especially should refrain from kissing, cuddling or even putting their arms round each other in public, as this could offend. Hand-shaking, however, is very common, even amongst close friends – this is a friendly gesture which cannot be misinterpreted.
- There are still some traces of old customs, such as Chinese women covering their mouths when they laugh or smile. This is because in olden days, women

were not supposed to laugh in public or show their teeth when they smiled.

- One major difference to note is the way in which Chinese people talk to someone they have just met. Where in the west our opening phrase might be 'Lovely day, isn't it?' or some other comment about the weather, the 'ice-breaker' of a Chinese person might be 'How old are you?' 'Are you married?' or 'How much do you earn?' (the answer to which would be something vague like 'Quite a lot' or 'Not very much'). The Chinese do not see these questions as personal, merely as a way of opening a conversation, so do not be offended by them. If you want to start a conversation yourself, but are unsure of how to go about it, simply smile and say 'hello'.

- Another point of etiquette: in the west it is considered good manners to apologise if you cough, sneeze or yawn. In China, however, these and other bodily functions are regarded as completely natural, and it is therefore not necessary to say anything.

- If you invite a Chinese friend out to dinner or to the cinema, it is generally taken for granted that you will pay for your guest. Be prepared to do this, unless you have made other arrangements beforehand, or you may find that your guest has arrived without any money.

- The Chinese place great importance on punctuality, and you should make every effort to arrive on time, especially if you have been invited for a meal. If your host says 'seven o'clock', that means that meal will be ready at that time. It is not acceptable to arrive at a meal or party half-an-hour or an hour late.

You may hear:	
你多大了？	**How old are you?**
Nǐ duō dà le?	
你结婚了吗？	**Are you married?**
Nǐ jiéhūn le ma?	

有朋友了吗？ *Yǒu péngyou le ma?*	**Have you got a girl/boyfriend?**
你在中国工作吗？ *Nǐ zài zhōngguó gōng zuò ma?*	**Are you working in China?**
你喜欢中国吗？ *Nǐ xǐhuān zhōngguó ma?*	**Do you like China?**
您在这做什么？ *Nín zài zhè zuò shénme?*	**What are you doing here?**
您上哪去？ *Nín shàng nǎr qù?*	**Where are you going?**
您去过 ... 吗？ *Nín qù guò... ma?*	**Have you been to ...?**
工资多少？ *Gōngzi duōshao?*	**How much is your salary?**

I am married	结了 *Jié le*
I'm not married	没结 *Méi jié*
I've got a girl/boyfriend	有朋友 *Yǒu péngyou*
I don't have a girl/boyfriend	没有朋友 *Méiyǒu péngyou*
I'm a teacher	我是教书的 *Wǒ shì jiāoshū de*
I'm a businessman/woman	我是商人 *Wǒ shì shāngrén*

Invitation to dinner

I hope I am not late	我没来晚吧？ *Wǒ méi lái wǎn ba?*
I've brought you a small present	这是给你的一个小礼物 *Zhèshì géi nǐ de yíge xiǎo lǐwù*

This is my ...	这是我 *Zhèshì wǒ ...*
... wife	夫人 *... fūren*
... husband	丈夫 *... zhàngfu*
... daughter	女儿 *... nǚér*
... son	儿子 *... érzi*
... father	母亲 *... mǔqin*
... mother	父亲 *... fùqin*
... boyfriend	男朋友 *... nán péngyou*
... girlfriend	女朋友 *... nǚ péngyou*
... family	家人 *... jiāren*

I can't eat any more, I've had enough	我吃不下了 *Wǒ chī búxià le*
It's late, I have to go	时间不早了，我得走了 *Shíjiān bù zǎo le, wó děi zǒu le*
Thank you for having us	谢谢你们的招待 *Xièxie nǐmen de zhāodài*
I hope we'll meet again	我希望我们能再见面 *Wǒ xīwàng wǒmen néng zài jiànmiàn*
Give my regards to ...	向 ... 问好 *Xiàng ... wènhǎo*
It was a wonderful evening	晚上过得很愉快 *Wǎnshang guòde hěnyùkuài*

You may hear:

请坐吧 *Qǐngzuòba*	**Please sit down**
请不要客气 *Qǐng búyào kèqi*	**Make yourself /yourselves at home**
喝白酒还是啤酒? *Hē báijiǔ háishì píjiǔ*	**Do you drink Chinese wine or beer?**
吃呀, 再吃呀! *Chī ya, zài chī ya*	**Please help yourself to more**
还想吃点什么吗? *Hái xiǎng chī diǎn shénme ma?*	**Would you like anything else?**
有空再来玩儿 *Yǒu kòng zài lái wánr*	**Please come again**
给我们写信来 *Géi wǒmen xiěxìn lái*	**Write to us**
一路平安! *Yílù píngān*	**Have a good trip**

Welcome meetings

- These can occur before any occasion, and can take the form of anything from a cocktail party to a very formal meeting. The latter may consist of guests being applauded as they enter, shaking hands with the dignitaries present and having ceremonial photos taken.

- On more informal occasions, there may be singing, dancing and even some impromptu poetry recitations to welcome the guests. If you know you are going to attend one of these meetings, it would be wise to prepare a party piece of your own, as guests are sometimes invited to perform too.

- It is on occasions like these that exchanging gifts (see page 50) is very common.

61

You may hear:	
Here is ..., who's going to ...	欢迎 ... 给我们 ... *Huānyíng ... gěi wǒmen ...*
... sing us a song	唱歌 *... chànggē*
... dance for us	跳舞 *... tiàowǔ*
... give us a performance	表演 *... biǎoyǎn*

I'm not very good at singing	我不会唱歌 *Wǒ búhuì chànggē*
May I dance instead?	跳舞行不行？ *Tiàowǔ xíng bùxíng?*

You may hear:	
我们只有一个小礼物送给表达我们的感激之情 *Wǒmen zhǐyǒu yíge xiǎo lǐwu sònggěi biǎodá wǒmen de gǎnjì zhīqíng*	We have this small present for you as an expression of our gratitude

I also have a souvenir for you	我也有一件纪念品给你们。 *Wǒ yěyǒu yíjiàn jìniàn pǐn géi nǐmen*
I really like the people here	我真喜欢这里的人 *Wǒ zhēn xǐhuān zhèlide rén*
Thank you for arranging this	感谢你们的安排 *Gǎnxiè nǐménde ānpái*

Business expressions

- If you are visiting China on business, you will probably find that your hosts speak at least some English. However, a few phrases in Chinese will always make a good impression.
- Most offices and factories will have some sort of security gate through which you will have to pass, so make sure that you have some identification with you.

I am ...	我是 ... *Wǒ shì ...*
Here is my card	我有名片 *Wǒ yǒu míngpiàn*
I'm here to see ...	我要见 ... *Wǒ yào jiàn ...*
General manager	总经理 *Zǒng jīnglǐ*
Responsible person	负责人 *Fùzérén*

In the street

- The Chinese are much less reticent about stopping strangers in the street than westerners. You may be stopped for various reasons: students trying to find someone willing to sponsor their studies abroad, people who want to practise their English, black-market traders trying either to sell you something or to offer to exchange money as a means of obtaining valuable 'hard' currencies, or even people who are simply curious about your appearance. The easiest way to avoid difficult situations is to keep walking, but with a smile and a shake of the head. Be very wary of giving your home address or telephone number to anyone you meet like this.

You may hear:

换钱吗？
Huàn qián ma?
Do you want to exchange money?

要帮忙吗？
Yào bāngmáng ma?
Do you need any help?

你们来旅游吗？
Nǐmen lái lǚyóu ma?
Are you tourists?

你们在这呆多久？
Nǐmen zàizhe dāi duōjiǔ?
How long are you staying here?

你住哪个宾馆？
Nǐ zhù nǎge bīnguǎn?
Which hotel are you staying in?

你的电话号码是多少？
Nǐde diànhuà hàomǎ shì duōshao?
What is your telephone number?

No (I don't want to exchange money)	不换 *Bú huàn*
We're staying here for two days	我们在这呆两天 *Wǒmen zàizhè dāi liǎng tiān*
Sorry, I don't know	对不起，我不知道 *Duì bùqǐ, wǒ bù zhīdào*
Do you like this city?	你喜欢这座城市吗？ *Nǐ xǐhuan zhè zuǒ chéngshì ma?*
Very much	非常喜欢 *Fēicháng xǐhuan*
Have you got used to the climate here?	你适应这里的天气吗？ *Nǐ shìyīng zhèlide tiānqì ma?*
Yes, but it's a bit dry	是的。只是有一点干燥 *Shìde. Zhǐshì yǒu yìdiǎn gānzào*

HEALTH

- China is famed for its traditional medicines which are based on natural herbs and techniques and which cure the root of the illness rather than just treat the symptoms. The most famous of these techniques are probably acupuncture and massage, which are reputed to cure even cancer and paralysis. Most major cities, however, have hospitals with a section for foreigners where western medicine is practised and English is spoken. In less extreme cases, you will probably find that your hotel has some provision for minor illness. You will be charged for all medical treatment received in China, so it may be wise to take out health insurance before you set off.
- One final word of warning: almost all Chinese are Rhesus positive blood group, so if you are in the unfortunate position of needing a blood transfusion, make sure that the doctors know your blood group.

Symptoms

I am ill	我病了 *Wǒ bìngle*
I want to see a doctor	我要看医生 *Wǒ yào kàn yīshēng*
I've got a temperature	我发烧 *Wǒ fāshāo*
I've had a cold	感冒了 *Gǎnmào le*
I feel very weak	我全身没力气 *Wǒ quánshēn méi lìqì*

I have ...	我 *Wǒ ...*

... diarrhoea	拉肚子 *... lā dùzi*
... a headache	头痛 *... tóutòng*
... a sore throat	嗓子疼 *... sǎngzi téng*
... a cough	咳嗽 *... késou*
... diabetes	有糖尿病 *... yǒu táng niào bìng*
... asthma	有气喘病 *... yǒu qì chuǎn bìng*

I feel dizzy	我头晕 *Wǒ tóuyūn*
I've had a heart attack	我心脏病犯了 *Wǒ xīnzàngbìng fàn le*
I've got an allergy	我过敏 *Wǒ guòmǐn*

I'm pregnant	我怀孕了 *Wǒ huáiyùn le*
I feel sick	我恶心 *Wǒ ěxin*
I've been sick	我吐了 *Wǒ tù le*
I'm bleeding	我流血 *Wǒ liúxuè*
I've fallen	我摔了一跤 *Wǒ shuāile yì jiāo*
I can't move this	这里不能动 *Zhèli bùnéng dòng*
It hurts here	我这里痛 *Wǒ zhèli tòng*

You may hear:

你哪儿不舒服？ *Nǐ nǎr bù shūfu?*	**What seems to be the matter?**
请躺下 *Qǐng tǎngxià*	**Lie down**
请把衣服脱下来 *Qǐng bǎ yīfu tuō xiàlai*	**Take off your coat**
请坐起来 *Qǐng zuò qǐlai*	**Sit up**
请把嘴张开 *Qǐng bǎ zuǐ zhāngkāi*	**Open your mouth**
请深呼吸 *Qǐng shēn hūxī*	**Breath deeply**
这儿疼吗？ *Zhèr téngma?*	**Does it hurt here?**
请到 X 光室 *Qǐng dào X guāng shì*	**Please go to the X-ray room**
请穿衣吧 *Qǐng chuān yī ba*	**Get dressed, please**

我给你开药
Wǒ gěi nǐ kāiyào

I'll give you a prescription

吃中药吗？
Chī zhōngyào ma?

Do you take Chinese medicine?

卧床休息几天吧
Wòchuáng xiūxi jǐtiān ba

Stay in bed for a few days

没断，是脱臼
Méiduàn, shì tuōjiù

Your bone is not broken, it is dislocated

这药一天吃三次
Zhè yào yìtiān chī sāncì

Take the medicine three times a day

饭后三十分钟服用
Fànhòu sānshí fēnzhōng fúyòng

Half an hour after each meal

有炎症
Yǒu yánzhèng

There is an infection

Treatment

I (don't) want traditional Chinese medicine

我（不）吃中药
Wǒ (bù) chī zhōngyào

I'd prefer western treatment

我吃西药
Wǒ chī xīyào

May I have acupuncture treatment?

能针灸吗？
Néng zhēnjiǔ ma?

How many pills should I take?

一次吃几丸/粒？
Yícì chī jǐwán?

I'm allergic to penicillin

我对盘尼西林过敏。
Wǒ duì pánníxīlín guòmǐn

Is the bone broken?

我的骨头断了吗？
Wǒ de gútou duàn le ma?

Do I need an operation?

要动手术吗？
Yào dòng shǒushù ma?

Can I have the operation at home?	我回国动手术行吗？ *Wǒ huí guó dòng shǒushù xíng ma?*
Please could you contact my Embassy	请帮我与我国大使馆联系一下 *Qǐng bāng wǒ yú wǒguó dàshǐguǎn liánxì yíxià*
I feel much better	我好多了 *Wó hǎo duō le*
I still feel bad	还不好 *hái bùhǎo*
Is it serious?	严重吗？ *Yán zhòng ma?*
Do I need to take any medication?	我需要用药吗？ *Wǒ xūyào yòng yào ma?*

At the dentist

● Chinese dentistry is not as advanced as in the west. Dentists are more or less unheard of in small towns and villages, where the people see toothache as a fact of life, albeit a painful one. In the city, however, dentistry is a growth business, and people often start queueing in the early hours for an appointment. Foreign tourists, however, should go to one of the large hospitals where there is usually a special department for them.

My tooth hurts a lot	我牙痛得很 *Wǒ yá tòng dé hěn*
Will I have to have the tooth out?	牙要拔掉吗？ *Yá yào bádiào ma?*
Can you fill it?	这颗牙能补吗？ *Zhè kē yá néng bǔ ma?*
I don't want to have the tooth out	我不想把它拔掉 *Wǒ bùxiǎng bǎ tā bádiào*
Can you give me something for the pain?	请帮我止痛吧 *Qǐng bāng wǒ zhǐtòng ba*

You may hear:

我先给你消炎 *Wǒ xiān géi nǐ xiāoyán*	I'll get rid of the swelling
我把它补上 *Wó bǎ tā bǔshang*	I'll fill the tooth
后天再来一次 *Hòutiān zàilái yícì*	Come back the day after tomorrow

Emergencies

Help!	帮忙/救命！ *Bāngmáng/jiùmìng!*
I've had a fall	我摔了一跤 *Wǒ shuāile yìjiāo*
I can't move my ...	不能动 *... bùnéng dòng*
leg	腿 *Tuǐ*
arm	胳臂 *Gēbei*
back/waist	腰 *Yáo*
hand	手 *Shǒu*
foot	脚 *Jiǎo*
Call an ambulance quickly	快叫救护车 *Kuài jiào jiùhùchē*
Find someone who can speak English	叫一个懂英语的人来 *Jiào yíge dǒng yīngyǔ de rén lái*
Is this the emergency room?	这是急诊室吗？ *Zhè shì jízhěnshì ma?*

At the chemist

- In China, contraceptives are available to married couples and to foreigners employed in China through the Family Planning Organisation. Foreign tourists, however, can usually buy condoms in most chemist shops.
- Most Chinese find anything concerning sex embarrassing, so it is best to be as discreet as possible when purchasing items such as contraceptives or tampons.
- Most medicines can be purchased over the counter without a prescription.

I want to buy ...	我要买 *Wǒ yào mǎi ...*
... aspirin	阿司匹林 ... *āsīpǐlín*
... eye drops	眼药水 ... *yǎnyàoshuǐ*
... throat lozenges	喉片 ... *hóupiàn*
... decongestant	感冒药 ... *gǎnmào yào*
... cough sweets	咳嗽药 ... *késouyào*
... indigestion tablets	胃痛药 ... *wèitòng yào*
... anti-diarrhoea tablets	止泻药 ... *zhǐxiè yào*
... pain killers	止痛药 ... *zhǐtòng yào*
... laxatives	轻泻剂 ... *qīngxiè jì*
... sleeping pills	安眠药 ... *ānmiányào*

... a thermometer	体温计
	... *tǐwēn jì*
... royal jelly	人参蜂王浆
	... *rénshēn fēngwáng jiāng*
... condoms	避孕套
	... *bìyùn tào*

You may see:	
急诊室	emergency room
jízhěnshì	
医院	hospital
yīyuàn	
医疗所	clinic
yīliáosuǒ	
药店	pharmacy
yàodiàn	

Have you got something for ...?	你有治 ... 的药吗？
	Ní yǒu zhì ... de yào ma?
... a headache	头痛
	... *tóutòng* ...
... a stomach upset	胃痛
	... *wèitòng* ...
... an insect bite ...	虫咬
	... *chóngyǎo* ...
a mosquito bite	蚊咬
	... *wényǎo* ...
... toothache ...	牙痛
	... *yá tòng* ...
Have you got any moth repellant?	你有防蛀剂吗？
	Nǐ yǒu fángzhùjì ma?

TRAVEL

- You are bound to want to travel during your stay in China: in such a vast, mysterious country, there is so much to see that the problem will be choosing what to include on a limited itinerary. You should plan your trip to make the most of your time: the best way to do this is to join a group of travellers and follow an organised route. Travelling alone in China is not always easy, and you may be regarded with some suspicion.
- China has made considerable progress in communications and transportation in recent years. A complete transport network of air, water and land has been developed, bringing all parts of the country within easy access.
- China has over 50,000 kilometres of railways, and about 900,000 kilometres of roads. Railways now reach all the provinces and autonomous regions with the exception of Xizang (Tibet). Of China's railways, over 25 per cent run in the western half of the country.

Travel Agencies

China International Travel Service

- This travel service specializes in arranging tours for foreign tourists and has branches in more than 100 Chinese cities. It deals mainly with package tours and commissioned services. Their package tours provide tourists with a comprehensive deal, including accommodation, transport, meals, sightseeing visits to places of interest with a guide and interpreter. There is a flat charge for this service, which is agreed in advance. Commissioned services enable tourists to choose the individual services they need. These include guides and interpreters, arrival and departure services, national and international travel arrangements, storage and transporting of luggage, purchasing tickets, applying for exit or transit visas, ordering taxis and applying for customs declarations and inspections. Tickets usually have to be booked through the CITS – your hotel will help you with this.

China Travel Service

- China Travel Service is the organization which receives tourists of Chinese origin (ie foreign nationals, nationals of Hong Kong, Macao, Taiwan etc). The CTS organizes group tours and provides these tourists with services similar to those of the China International Travel Service. The CTS has local offices in many cities.

Trains and Buses

- These are the most common means of transport in China, and are usually cheap, reliable but very crowded.
- There are three types of train:
  - slow, which cover short distances, stopping at all stations.
  - medium, which connect the main towns and cities in China

- fast, which provide an express service between Peking (Beijing) and Canton (Guangzhou) and certain other major centres.
- The Chinese do not have first and second class tickets, but divide the seats and berths into hard and soft. 'Hard-seat' compartments have wooden benches on which the travellers sit, or stretch out if there's room. Soft seats are usually together in one compartment and are always available for foreign travellers. Hard berths are triple-decker beds (about 50 or 60 to a compartment) with pillows and blankets provided. Soft berths are double-decker beds (four to a compartment) and offer the traveller much better service and more privacy.
- Stations can be readily identified by their name (which consists of the name of the town plus 站 *zhàn*, so Peking station is 北京站 *Běijīngzhàn*), the large clock and the crowds of travellers and all their paraphernalia.
- Child discounts operate according to height, not age: under 1m tall (just over 3ft), children travel free. Between 1m and 1.3m they pay a quarter of the adult fare. Over this height, they must pay full fare.
- Tickets are usually inspected upon entering and leaving the station. There are no ticket inspectors on board.
- Buses run within the cities and also provide a limited service between cities.
- The best way to ensure you don't get lost on the buses is to ask a Chinese person to write your destination and bus route in characters before you set off.
- Buses are always extremely crowded, especially during the rush hours. You will probably be pushed and shoved, and, although pickpockets are rare, it is wise to hang on to any bags you may have and make sure nothing is sticking out of your pockets, as you might drop something in the rush.
- There are few one-way streets in China, so you will usually find bus stops on both sides of the road. At the bus stop you will find a notice telling you the final destination of the bus, the stops it makes – *route* and the times of the first and last buses.

Where is the China International Travel Service?	国际旅行社在哪里？ *Guójì lǚxíngshè zài nǎli?*
Can I buy a map of the area?	能买到本地地图吗？ *Néng mǎi dào běndì dìtú ma?*
What is there to see here?	这里有什么名胜？ *Zhèli yǒu shénme míngshèng?*
Where can I get a train timetable?	哪里卖火车时刻表？ *Nǎli mài huǒchē shíkè biǎo?*

Where is ...	... 在哪里？ *... zài nǎli?*
... the station	火车站 *Huǒchēzhàn ...*
... bus stop	汽车站 *Qìchēzhàn ...*
... taxi rank	出租汽车 *Chūzūqìchē ...*

How much does it cost?	票价多少？ *Piàojià duōshao?*
Can you take a bus there?	坐公共汽车行吗？ *Zuò gōnggòng qìchē xíngma?*
Could you tell me how to get to ...?	请告诉我到 ... 怎么走？ *Qǐng gàosù wǒ dào ... zěnme zǒu?*
Where can I buy a ticket?	在哪儿买票？ *Zài nǎr mǎipiào?*
I'd like two tickets	我买两张票 *Wó mǎi liǎngzhāng piào*
What time does it leave?	车几点开？ *Chē jí diǎn kāi?*
How many stops are there?	多少站？ *Duōshao zhàn?*
Is it an express train or a local train?	是快车还是慢车？ *Shì kuàichē háishì mànchē?*

Must I change?	要换车吗？ *Yào huàn chē ma?*
What time does it arrive?	几点到？ *Jǐdiǎn dào?*
Which is the (dining car/sleeping car)?	几号车厢是 (餐车/卧铺车) ？ *Jǐhào chēxiāng shì (cānchē/wòpùchē)?*
Please could you tell me where to get off?	到站请告诉我 *Dào zhàn qǐng gàosu wǒ*

I would like a ... ticket	我要 ... 票 *Wǒ yào ... piào*
... single	单程 *... dānchéng*
... return	来回 *... láihuí*
... second class	普通 *... pǔtōng*
... first class	头等舱 *... tóuděngcāng*
... soft-berth	软卧 *... ruǎnwò*
... hard-berth	硬卧 *... yìngwò*

Is this the train to ...?	这是去 ... 的火车吗？ *Zhèshì qù ... de huǒchē ma?*
Which platform does it leave from?	在第几站台？ *Zài dìjǐ zhàntái?*

By plane

- Travelling around China by plane has become a lot more popular since an increase in rail fares made the price of a first-class rail ticket more expensive than a plane ticket.

77

- There are over 170 domestic civil aviation routes in China leading to over 80 of the larger cities and to the remote frontier regions. Direct air routes have been established between Beijing and all the provinces, municipalities and autonomous regions, with the exception of Taiwan Province. International or contingency airports at Beijing, Tianjin, Urumqi, Shanghai, Guangzhou, and Guilin can accommodate the large airliners. The Civil Aviation Administration of China (CAAC) operates 18 international air routes and has signed air agreements with over 40 countries. The CAAC has been increasing and modernizing its aircraft fleet in service. Boeing-747SP airliners have been used on international and domestic services since 1980. International airlines of most western countries operate services to China.

What time does the plane from ... to ... take off?	从 ... 到 ... 的飞机几点起飞？ *Cóng ... dào ... de fèijī jídiǎn qǐfēi?*
How many flights a week are there between ... and ...?	从 ... 到 ... 一周几次班机？ *Cóng ... dào ... yìzhōu jǐcì bānjī?*
Must I change plane?	要换飞机吗？ *Yào huàn fēijī ma?*
What time does the plane arrive?	飞机几点到？ *Fēijī jídiǎn dào?*

Hiring a bicycle

- Cycling is extremely popular in China – few people own a car, but almost everyone has a bicycle. It is one of the best ways to get around, as long as you remember to obey traffic regulations and keep to the right.
  It is possible to join groups of cyclists (minimum number 15) who have a national guide to escort the party from town to town where they are joined by a local guide.

I'd like to hire a bicycle	我想租一辆自行车 *Wó xiǎng zū yí liàng zìxíngchē*

May I borrow a pump?　借我一个打气筒可以吗？
Jiè wǒ yíge dǎqitǒng kéyǐ ma?

Could you fix a basket on it?　能安个车筐吗？
Néng ān ge chēkuāng ma?

May I return it a bit later?　我能晚一点还车吗？
Wǒ néng wǎnyìdiǎn huánchē me?

You may hear:

您租多长时间？
Nín zū duōcháng shíjiān?

How long do you want it for?

请交 ... 块押金
Qǐngjiāo ... kuài yājīn

Please leave a deposit of ... yuan

后天下午六点前请务必还车
Hòutiān xiàwǔ liùdiǎn qián qǐng wùbì huánchē

Please make sure you return the bike before 6pm the day after tomorrow

还车时，我会还你 ... 块钱
Huànchē shí, wǒhuì huán nǐ ... kuàiqián

I'll refund you the ... yuan when you return the bike

祝你一路顺风，先生
Zhù nǐ yílù shùnfēng, xiānsheng

Have a pleasant trip

I'd like to keep it for ...　我想借
wó xiǎng jiè

... two days　两天
... liǎngtiān

... a week　一周
... yìzhōu

... a couple of weeks　半个月
... bànge yuè

By boat

● If you are on the coast or near a river, travelling by boat is a pleasant, relaxing way to see more of China. Chinese boats don't have first-class sections, but second class is well-equipped and comfortable. Third-class accommodation is on the lower deck of the boat, and is usually noisy, crowded and not usually chosen by foreigners.

- China had many rivers, 400,000 kilometres of which are navigable. The 6300km Changjiang (Yangtze) River is the artery of China's inland navigation. Navigable routes on the Changjiang and its tributaries extend over 70,000 kilometres. Electronically controlled navigation signals have been set up along the river for round-the-clock navigation. The magnificence of scenery along the Three Gorges of the Changjiang River is a unique sight. A pleasure cruise on the beautiful Lijiang River from Guilin to Yangshuo has also been set up for tourists.

- There are many seaports along the coast of China's mainland. The major seaports include Dalian, Qinhuangdao, Tianjin, Yantai, Qingdao, Lianyungang, Shanghai, Ningbo, Fuzhou, Xiamen, Shantou, Huangpu and Zhanjiang. Linked with all major ports of the world, Shanghai, Tianjin, Guangzhou, Dalian are the starting ports of the ocean shipping routes.

Other forms of transport

- In large cities, the two most popular forms of public transport are taxis, which are much easier to find than they used to be, and small buses known as 'bread buses', which look like mini-buses. These are recommended for several reasons: firstly, they can be flagged down if there are still seats available; secondly, they will let you get off at the most convenient place for your destination; and finally they are a lot cheaper than taxis and easier to find.

- Double-decker buses are in use in some cities, but they are regarded as typically western.

- Stereotyped images of rickshaws are now out-dated in large cities although this form of transport is still used in smaller towns, mainly for goods and luggage.

- A few large cities have an underground (subway) system, but most places rely on buses.

TABLE OF RAILWAY DISTANCES BETWEEN MAJOR TOURIST CITIES
(IN KILOMETRES)

	BEIJING	SHANGHAI	TIANJIN	GUANGZHOU	NANNING	GUILIN	CHANGSHA	WUCHANG	NANJING	WUXI	SUSHOU	HANGZHOU	JINAN	QINGDAO	XI'AN	KUNMING	CHENGDU	CHONGQING	DALIAN
SHANGHAI	1462																		
TIANJIN	137	1325																	
GUANGZHOU	2313	1811	2450																
NANNING	2565	2063	2702	1334															
GUILIN	2134	1632	2271	903	431														
CHANGSHA	1587	1187	1724	726	978	547													
WUCHANG	1229	1534	1366	1084	1336	905	358												
NANJING	1157	305	1020	2116	2368	1937	1492	1229											
WUXI	1334	128	1197	2191	1939	1760	1315	1406	177										
SUZHOU	1376	86	1239	1897	2149	1718	1273	1448	219	42									
HANGZHOU	1651	189	1514	1622	1874	1443	998	1356	494	317	275								
JINAN	494	968	357	2284	2536	2105	1558	1200	663	840	882	1157							
QINGDAO	887	1361	750	2677	2929	2498	1951	1593	1056	1233	1275	1550	393						
XI'AN	1165	1511	1302	2129	2381	1950	1403	1045	1206	1383	1425	1700	1177	1570					
KUNMING	3179	2677	3316	2216	1501	1422	1592	1950	2982	2805	2763	2488	3119	3512	1942				
CHENGDU	2048	2185	2544	1829	1750	1920	1887	2048	2225	2267	2542	2019	2412	2805	842	1100			
CHONGQING	2552	2501	2689	2040	1325	1246	1416	1774	2552	2729	2771	2312	2523	2916	1346	1102	504		
DALIAN	1238	2426	1101	3551	3803	3372	2825	2467	2121	2298	2340	2615	1458	1851	2403	4417	3790	3286	
SHENYANG	841	2029	704	3154	3406	2975	2428	2070	1724	1901	1943	2218	1061	1454	2006	4020	3393	2889	397

A sightseeing guide

- The following is an extremely brief guide to places to visit in China. For more detailed descriptions and other possibilities, consult a guide book.
- Chinese travel agencies organise many tours each year, covering between five and nine cities in about two or three weeks. You can thus choose the route best suited to your interests and the time available to you. They will also be able to provide you with brochures to give you a clearer idea of which area to choose.

北京 *Běijīng* (Peking) is the capital of the People's Republic of China. Here are some of the main places of interest:

首都机场 *Shǒudū jīchǎng* (Capital Airport) is situated to the east of Peking.

北京站 *Běijīng zhàn* (Peking Railway Station) is in the heart of the city.

天安门广场 *Tiān'ānmén guángchǎng* (Tiananmen Square) is one of th largest squares in the world, the scene of the student unrest in May and June 1989 as well as the location for all official parades and military reviews.

天安门 *Tiān'ānmén* (Gate of Heavenly Peace) is on the north side of Tiananmen Square; from here, Mao Zedong announced the founding of the Republic, and it is considered as the symbol of new China by the people.

人民大会堂 *Rénmín dàhuìtáng* (the Great Hall of the People) stands to the west of the Square and is the seat of the National People's Congress. It contains enormous reception rooms and banqueting halls.

中国革命博物馆, 中国历史博物馆 *Zhōngguó gémìng bówùguǎn, zhōngguó lìshǐ bówùguǎn* (the Museum of Chinese History and of the Chinese Revolution) is situated to the east of the Square.

人民英雄纪念碑 *Rémín Yīngxióng jìniànbēi* (Monument to the People's Heroes) is on the south side of the Square.

毛主席纪念堂 *Máo zhǔxí jìniàntáng* (Chairman Mao Memorial Hall) is also on the south side of the the Square, beyond the monument.

故宫博物馆 *Gùgōng bówùguǎn* (Palace Museum), also known as Forbidden City, is located just north of Tiananmen Square and was built between 1406 and 1420 during the Ming Dynasty. It was the residence of the Ming and Qing emperors and is the largest and most integrated of China's remaining ancient palaces. It featured in the film 'The Last Emperor' and is open to the public every day from 8.30am to 4.30pm.

景山公园 *Jǐngshān gōngyuán* (Jingshan Park) was a royal garden during the Yuan, Ming and Qing Dynasties. It stands to the north of Palace Museum, and from the top of the Wanchun Pavilion you get an impressive panorama of the city.

北海公园 *Běihǎi gōngyuán* (Beihai Park) is located to the west of Jingshan Park. It was first built about 800 years ago, and was used as a royal garden by the Yuan , Ming and Qing Dynasties. The gardens are centred around the Beihai Lake and are typical of traditional Chinese landscape gardening.

天坛公园 *Tiāntán gōngyuán* (Temple of Heaven). The 38-metre-high Qinian Hall is built of wood without using a single nail, and is masterpiece of traditional Chinese architecture. There is also the Echo Wall, where two people standing at opposite ends can talk to each other without shouting.

颐和园 *Yíhé yuán* (Summer Palace) was formerly a palace of the emperors, but is now a park.

北京动物园 *Běijīng dòngwùyuán* (Beijing Zoo) where you can find over 5000 animals.

香山公园 *Xiāngshān gōngyuán* (Fragrant Hills Park) lies 557 metres above sea level. The best time to see it is in autumn when the maple leaves turn a fiery red.

长城 *Chángchéng* (the Great Wall) is more than 6350 kilometres long, rising and falling with the mountain ridges. It has an average height of 7.8 metres, and an average width of about 6 metres, allowing enough room for ten people or half a dozen horses to walk abreast.

十三陵 *Shísān líng* (Ming tombs). Thirteen imperial tombs of the Ming Dynasty.

中南海 *Zhōngnánhǎi* (Central and South Sea) houses China's highest-ranking leaders. The State Council's offices are located here. Some parts of the offices are open to the public from 9am to 5pm seven days a week.

Overnight Trips from Peking

承德 *Chéngdé* is a mountain resort which was used as a summer retreat for the Manchu Court during the Qing Dynasty.

北戴河 *Běidàihé* is a seaside resort.

山海关 *Shānhǎiguān* is known as the gateway to the Northeast (Manchuria). It is the point where the Great Wall meets the sea.

天津 *Tiānjīn* is nicknamed the East Gate of China. It is well known, both in China and abroad for its handicrafts, such as traditional Chinese New Year pictures, Yang Liu Qing paintings, painted clay figurines, kites and fine rugs and carpets. It is 120 kilometres from Beijing.

东北 *Dōngběi – the Northeast*

● In northeast China, known as Manchuria, there are three provinces.

哈尔滨 *Hā'ěrbīn* is the capital of Heilongjiang Province. The city's architecture shows a marked Russian influence, and every winter the annual snow and ice festival attracts many visitors with its beautiful ice sculptures and lights.

长春 *Chángchūn* is the capital of Jilin Province and the former capital of the last emperor, the 'puppet' Manzhouguo. Aixinjueluo Puyi was crowned here and had his palace and government buildings in the city.

Jilin Province has three specialities: ginseng, sable and

deer antler, which are known as the 'three treasures of the Northeast'.

沈阳 *Shěnyáng* is the capital of Liaoning Province. Before the Qing emperors took over the whole country, they had their imperial palace here. Dong Ling and Bei Ling are the tombs of the emperors and empresses. The Museum of Liaoning Province has over 3000 exhibits.

千山 *Qiān shān* (Mount Qian/Thousand Mountains) is a famous scenic spot in the Northeast, also known as the 'Pearl of the Northeast'. About 40 kilometres from here are hot springs where the water can reach 70°C.

大连 *Dàlián* is the third largest port in China, and is one of the best-known scenic resorts of the Northeast.

上海 – *Shànghǎi*

As one of the three municipalities directly under the Central Government, Shanghai is the largest city in China, with a rich history. It is the leading commercial and cultural centre of China and has important manufacturing and shipping industries too.

豫园 *Yù yuán* are gardens, originally belonging to an important family. They were built during the Ming Dynasty, from 1559 onwards, and some of the trees are over 4000 years old.

城隍庙 *Chénghuáng miào*, formerly a temple, is now a large bazaar including bird markets, bookstores, tea houses, restaurants, department stores etc. Frequented by locals and foreign visitors alike.

玉佛寺 *Yùfó sì* (Temple of Jade Buddha) was built in 1882 and measures 1.9 metres high and 1.3 metres wide.

龙华塔 (龙华寺) *Lónghuá tǎ* (*Lónghuá sì*). The focal point of this temple is a wooden pagoda over 40 metres tall.

黄浦公园 *Huángpú gōng yuán* (also known as Waitan Park). The Chinese people have only been allowed to enter these gardens since the Republic was founded.

上海动物园 *Shànghǎi dòngwùyuán* (Shanghai Zoo) contains many rare wild animals from China and other parts of the world.

上海植物园 *Shànghǎi zhíwùyuán (Shanghai Botanical Garden)* is famous for its miniature trees and its rock flowers and plants.

南京路 *Nánjīng lù* is a shopping centre, specialising in fashion.

浙江 – *Zhéjiāng Province*

杭州 *Hángzhōu* is the capital of the province with a history going back over 2000 years. It is one of the most attractive cities in China, hence the Chinese saying 'There is paradise in heaven, then there are Suzhou and Hangzhou on earth'. Xi Hu (West Lake) has over ten scenic spots and places of historical interest, and is referred to as 'paradise on earth' Hangzhou and Suzhou produce particularly fine silk and embroidered goods.

江苏 – *Jiāngsū Province*

南京 *Nánjīng* is the capital of the province. Eight dynasties made it their capital, and its history goes back over 2400 years. Dr Sun Yatsen had his presidential office here, and his tomb is in the Purple Mountains to the east of the city. Here you can also see the tomb of Emperor Taizu, the founder of the Ming Dynasty. An attraction of a different kind is the Great Changjiang Bridge at Nanjing, which is over 6½ kilometres long. Trains, trucks, cars and pedestrians all cross the bridge in different ways.

无锡 *Wúxī* is located on the shores of Lake Tai and is surrounded by beautiful natural scenery.

苏州 *Sūzhōu* is renowned for its landscape gardens, of which there were already 200 by the time of the Qing Dynasty. Hu Qiu is an especially beautiful place. Suzhou is sometimes called the 'Venice of the Orient'.

安徽 – *Ānhūi Province*

黄山 *Huáng shān* (The Huang Mountains) have 72 peaks, and there are four things which make them unique: the rare pine trees, the unusual rock formations, the seas of clouds which surround them and the hot springs.

九华山 *Jiǔhuá shān* (Mount Jiuhua) is one of the four great Buddhist mountains in China. There are more than 70 temples and 6000 Buddhist sculptures in what is described as the temple forest. These peaceful and secluded mountains are marked by the incense smoke rising from them.

福建 – *Fújiàn Province*

● Fujian is the province bordering Taiwan, with only the Taiwan Straits separating them. Its capital is Fuzhou.

厦门 *Xiàmén* is known as the 'garden on the sea', and is one of the special economic zones, established by the government to encourage foreign investment.

泉州 *Quánzhōu* is a cultural city with a long history and a famous port. During the Song and Yuan Dynasties, Quanzhou and the Egyptian port of Alexandria vied for the position as the largest trade port in the world.

武夷山 *Wǔyí shān* is said to be the most beautiful mountain range in the south-east. Its 36 peaks have many amazing caves and rock formations.

江西 – *Jiāngxī Province*

庐山 *Lú shān* is a mountain summer resort. Its towering peaks, mountain springs and waterfalls and cool summer weather along with its breathtaking scenery have made this spot very popular with Chinese and foreigners alike.

景德镇 *Jǐngdézhèn* is known as the capital of porcelain: its china is famed throughout the world.

山东 – *Shāndōng Province*

济南 *Jǐnán* is over 2600 years old and is known as China's 'City of Fountains': there are so many springs and fountains that there is almost one for every family. The spring waters converge on the Daming Lake, which makes the area a popular beauty spot.

泰山 *Tài shān* (Mount Tai) is the most important of China's five sacred mountains. Many of the ancient emperors went there to hold ceremonies before their coronations, worshipping Heaven and Earth. The Dai Temple at the foot of the mountain has a mural over 60 metres long, depicting more than 650 lively figures, all different from one another.

曲阜 *Qūfǔ* is the hometown of Confucius, one of ancient China's great philosophers. The Confucian Temple and other historic sites provide the visitor with a vivid glimpse into the past.

青岛 *Qīngdǎo* is a sea-port and holiday resort, well-known for its European architecture and Qingdao beer, produced in a factory first set up by the Germans.

崂山 *Láo shān* (Mount Lao) has a miraculous spring whose water level remains the same throughout the year, neither overflowing in the rainy season nor drying up in drought. The mineral water from it is fragrant and sweet, and is very popular with visitors to the mountain.

河南 – *Hénán Province*

郑州 *Zhèngzhōu*, the capital, dates back to 559 AD. There are many things to see and do here, including trips on the Huanghe (Yellow River), the ruins of an ancient city from the Shang Dynasty and relics from the Yangshao Culture.

嵩山 *Sōng shān*. This mountain range has over 70 individual peaks, the highest being almost 1500 metres. The Shaolin Temple, built in 495 AD was one of the birthplaces of Buddhism. The Shaolin martial arts are highly regarded in China and Southeast Asia.

洛阳 *Luòyáng* was the capital city of nine dynasties between 559 AD and 1720, and so there are many places of historical interest to visit, including gardens and villas which belonged to the ruling lords and officials. Luoyang's other claim to fame is its peonies: it boasts 150 varieties, including the very valuable Erqiao. Even if you are not interested in horticulture, these beautiful flowers are well worth a visit.

开封 *Kāifēng* is one of the six ancient capitals of China. Tie Ta (the Iron Pagoda) on the outskirts of the city is over 1000 years old and is made of glass blocks coloured red by iron oxide. The pagoda is octagonal and has thirteen levels, standing almost 55 metres tall.

济公山 *Jìgōng shān* (Mount Jigong) is known as the 'Garden in the Sky'.

湖北 – *Húběi Province*

武汉 *Wǔhàn* is the capital of the province and is divided into three by the Changjiang (Yangtse) and Han Rivers. The Dong Hu (East Lake) is nearly four times the size of its sister lake (Xi Hu) in Hangzhou (see page 84), and is the perfect place for a leisurely stroll.

武当山 *Wǔdāng shān* is the mountain seat of Taoism. Ancient buildings and temples stretch for almost 30 kilometres along the range, most dating back to the fifteenth century. Perhaps the most eye-catching of these is the glittering 'Golden Palace.'

湖南 – *Húnán Province*

Hunan Province has produced many of China's revolutionaries: Mao Zedong, Liu Shaoqi, Peng Dehuai, He Long and Tao Zhu during the last sixty years and Tan Sitong, Huang Xing and Cai E before that, to name but a few. Nowadays, the province is still renowned for its celebrities, but they tend to be artists, dramatists and other people from the art world.

长沙 *Chángshā* is the capital of the province and is over 3000 years old. The city is best known for its beautiful scenery and its archeological sites, including the Han Dynasty tombs on the outskirts of the city where an almost perfectly preserved female corpse dating back over 3000 years was discovered.

张家界 *Zhāngjiājiè* is also know as the Qingyan Mountain. This area of mountains and lakes is a national forest park.

广东 – *Guǎngdōng (Kwangtung) Province*

广州 *Guǎngzhōu*. In 214 BC, the first Chinese emperor founded the town of Nanhai, and it is on this site that the present-day city of Guangzhou now stands, only three hours by train from Hong Kong. Guangzhou was the source of the revolution which led to the overthrow of the Qing Dynasty, but nowadays it is better known as the home of Cantonese cooking.

越秀山公园 *Yuèxiùshān gōngyuán* is Guangzhou's best-known park, and has three man-made lakes and a wide variety of trees, in addition to several historic buildings and sites.

兰圃 *Lánpǔ* lie to the west of Yuexiu Park and are also known as the 'Gardens of Orchids', as the gardens have over 10,000 orchids of many different varieties.

白云山 *Báiyún shān* literally means 'white cloud mountains', and although the mountains are not as high as this seems to imply, it is still a breathtakingly beautiful place to visit, with spectacular views and historical sites.

佛山 *Fó shān* is 28 kilometres from Guangzhou and dates back over 1300 years. It is famous for its pottery, porcelain, textiles and other crafts.

丛化温泉 *Cónghuà wēnquán*. There are twelve hot springs at Conghua whose temperatures range from 36°C to one at 71°C. The resort is very popular and tends to get crowded, especially at weekends.

深圳 *Shēnzhèn* is a fast-growing, modern city which owes much of its development to its border with Hong Kong. It is another of the government's special economic zones.

珠海 *Zhūhǎi*. This city on the coast actually consists of 112 islands, connected by land to Macao on one side and by sea to Hong Kong on the other. It is a thriving port, and the lively bustle and mild weather attract tourists. The city is also notable for its varied styles of architecture.

四川 – *Sìchuān Province*

成都 *Chéngdū* was a capital city as early as 2200 years ago. It is called the 'land of abundance' because the mild climate and fertile land combine to make the area's agricultural output one of the highest in China. The many historic sites are linked with famous poets, emperors and religions.

九寨沟 *Jiǔzhàigōu* is one of two spectacular nature reserves in the province, situated due north of Chengdu. It has beautiful forests and lakes, earning it the name of 'World of Fairy Tales', but it is quite isolated and difficult to reach.

乐山大佛 *Lèshān dà fó*. Fo means 'Buddha' and *da* means 'big' or 'great' and the reason for this combination will be obvious when you arrive in Leshan, because the famous statue of Buddha, carved into the sandstone cliff, is truly colossal, some say the biggest in the world. The statue's head reaches the top of the mountain, its feet rest beside the river and are big enough for a hundred people to sit on them. Even his nose is over five metres long!

峨嵋山 *Éméi shān* is the highest of the Buddhist mountains and provides a natural museum, with perfect conditions for the plant and animal life living there. There can be a temperature difference of 15°C between the bottom of the mountain, where it is like spring, and the top, where it is freezing cold. You should not attempt to climb it without a guide, as several parts of the path are dangerous.

重庆 *Chóngqìng* is a very attractive city in the mountains with a history going back over 3000 years. It is sometimes called 'Foggy Chongqing', due to the mists which sweep down into the river valley. It was the provincial capital of the Chinese nationalists.

长江三峡 *Chángjiáng sān xiá* are three gorges along the Changjiang (Yangtse) River. They stretch for a total of 120 miles and the best way to see them is from a boat; there are regular cruises down the Changjiang, often lasting several days.

贵州 – *Guìzhōu Province*

● Maotai wine is made in this region and is one of the better-known Chinese wines.

黔灵山 *Qiánlíng shān*. Lying to the southwest of Guiyang, the capital city, the Qianling mountain range is said to be the most beautiful in the region, with its towering peaks, temples, pine trees, caves, natural springs and pools, Buddhist sculpture and lakes and flowers.

黄果树瀑布 *Huángguǒshù pùbù* are amazing waterfalls at Huangguoshu, and are very popular with tourists.

云南 – *Yúnnán Province*

Yunnan borders Burma , Laos and Vietnam, and has a very mild climate. There are many minority groups in the region, especially near the borders.

昆明 *Kūnmíng* is the capital of the province and is over 2000 years old. The best-known attractions in this 'City of Spring' are the Xishan Park and the Dian and Green lakes.

大理 *Dàlǐ* is known as the 'Switzerland of the East', due to the snowy peaks of the Cang Mountains.

西双版纳 *Xīshuāngbǎnnà* is a tropical region known as the 'Green Pearl', inhabited by the Dai people, whose lifestyle and customs are fascinating. Although remote, Xishuangbanna is well worth a visit.

石林 *Shílín* is the 'Forest of Rocks', an incredibly beautiful natural labyrinth of rocks, inhabited by the Sani people.

陕西 – *Shǎnxi Province*

西安 *Xī'ān*, still the capital of the province, was the capital of twelve dynasties over a period of 1000 years. It was one of the birthplaces of ancient Chinese culture and the famous Silk Road started here. The first emperor of China is buried here in a still unexcavated tomb, guarded by an army of more than 7000 terracotta warriors, horses and chariots. This amazing discovery, made in 1974, is still being unearthed, and some of the figures have been exhibited around the world. The site is open to visitors, but you will have to pay a fee if you want to take photos. Ancient China is vividly brought to life in Xi'an: the Forest of Steles, the Bell Tower , the two Wild Geese Pagodas, the Huaqing hot springs and the 6000-year-old neolithic village (now a museum) at Banpo all contribute to this.

华山 *Huá shān* is one of the most imposing mountains in China, and one of the most difficult to climb.

甘肃 – *Gānsù Province*

- The Silk Road runs through Gansu Province for almost 1600 kilometres. The Mogao Caves at Dunhuang date back to the 4th century and have almost 500 separate caverns, with many sculptures and frescoes. The caves in the Maiji Mountain are said to be the 'greatest gallery of sculptures in the East'.

青海 – *Qīnghǎi Province*

西宁 *Xīníng* is the province's capital city and the South Silk Road starts here. You will also find the Dongguan Mosque, the 'greatest mosque in the northwest', built over 500 years ago. Taser Lamasery, 25 kilometres from the city, is one of the best-known lamaseries (lama monasteries) in China.

山西 – *Shānxī Province*

太原 *Tàiyuán* is the capital city and is very old. Even the local wine dates back 1400 years! It is, incidentally, one of the most popular wines in China. The Jin Temple dates back to 771 BC and the nearby hot spring maintains a constant temperature all year round.

大同 *Dàtóng*. The Yungang Grotto, 16 kilometres from the city, has over 50 caves with thousands of stone carvings and sculptures. Sakamuni Buddha's life story is told in a series of stone carvings.

五台山 *Wǔtái shān* is another of the four famous Buddhist Mountains, and is nicknamed the 'cool mountain'.

- The following provinces are known as 'Autonomous Regions': there are several of these in China, and they should always be referred to as such, to avoid offending people.

广西 – *Guǎngxī Zhuàng Autonomous Region*

南宁 *Nánníng* is the region's capital and has a sub-tropical climate, so the weather is usually pleasant all year round. There are plenty of parks and scenic spots for walks and picnics, and to the north of the city are the famous rocks of Yiling. These spectacular formations attract visitors from all over the world.

桂林 *Guìlín* is described by some as the loveliest landscape in China. Its limestone mountains and sense of mystery have attracted tourists for hundreds of years: the best way to appreciate it is to take a boat trip down the Li River. The national park here looks exactly like a traditional Chinese landscape painting, and there is no end of things to amaze visitors: mountain peaks, caves, underground rivers, stalactites and stalagmites shaped like animals and beautiful rock formations. Fubo Mountain in the northeast and Ludi Yan in the northwest are also places of great natural beauty.

阳朔 *Yángshuò* rivals Guilin as a place of scenic beauty, and it is usually less crowded.

西藏 – *Xīzàng Autonomous Region (Tibet)*

拉萨 *Lāsà*, the capital of the region, dates back more than 1300 years and lies 12,000 feet above sea level. The Potala Palace is a thirteen storey building set on a cliff, and was first built in the 7th century.

宁夏 – *Níngxià Huí Autonomous Region*

- The capital city of Yinchuan is near the Yellow River, at the foot of Mount Helan. The city has some places of interest quite different from other Chinese cities, such as the tombs of the Xixia emperors, which are called the Pyramid of China, and the One-Hundred-and-Eight Pagodas at Qingtongxia Reservoir, which are the only large group of pagodas in China. The city is over 1000 years old and is inhabited by the Hui people, one of the minority nations.

新疆 – *Xīnjiāng Uygur Autonomous Region*

乌鲁木齐 *Wūlǔmùqí* is the capital of this region and the home to thirteen minority people. Tianchi, the 'Lake of Heaven', is well worth a visit, and tourists can also visit the Tianshan Pastureland, 75 kilometres from the city. Here you can spend some time with Kazak families, sample their special tea served with water melon and watch their horse races and other local sports.

吐鲁番 *Tǔlǔfān* is an oasis in a desert: it is located in a geographical depression and lies 500 feet below sea level. It is nicknamed the 'desert of heat' as the temperature can rise to 48°C in summer. Tulufan (also known as Turpan) was an important point on the Silk Road, and its raisins are some of the best in the world.

千佛洞 *Qiānfódòng* is the site of the Thousand Buddha Caves.

内蒙古 – *Inner Mongolia Autonomous Region*

呼和浩特 *Hūhéhàotè*. The Mongolian people call their capital city the 'green city'. It has quite a few places of interest, including the largest horse-racing course in China.

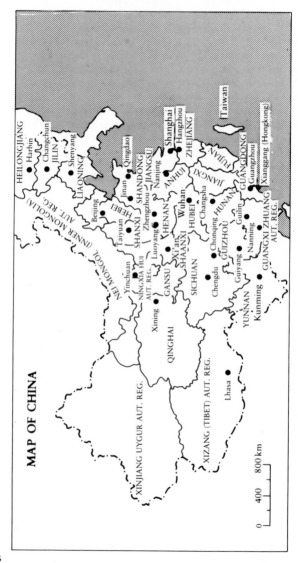

MAP OF CHINA

SHOPPING

• Generally speaking, foreigners can do their shopping in three different types of shops:

• Friendship Stores, which were established to sell high-quality goods to foreigners. Payment must be made in Foreign Exchange Certificates (see page 118 for details about these) as local currency is not accepted.

• Department stores and shops: these can be owned by the state, conglomerates or private individuals. They provide an interesting insight into everyday life in China: you will see the Chinese doing their shopping, queuing and fighting over the sought-after goods and carrying large loads of shopping home on their bikes.

• Free markets, which sell a wide range of food, handicrafts, clothes and furnishings. It is acceptable to bargain in the markets (not anywhere else) although this must be done politely – it is not like 'haggling' in the Middle Eastern markets.

- 店 *diàn* is the general word for shop, and is often found after a noun indicating the type of shop.
- Chinese people do not normally ask for receipts unless they are buying something in connection with work. You should always ask for a receipt for customs purposes, especially with large purchases. Chinese receipts are characterised by a large red seal.

Please could I have ...?	请给我 *Qǐng gěi wǒ ...*
... a receipt	收据 *... shōujù*
... two more bags	两个袋子 *... liǎngge dàizi*

You may hear:

袋子要收钱 *Dàizi yào shōuqián*	**Bags are not free**
收据在这 *Shōujù zàizhè*	**Here is your receipt**

Shops

department store	百货商店/百货公司 *bǎihuò shāngdiàn/bǎihuò* *gōngsī*
bookshop	书店 *shūdiàn*
antique shop	古董店/古玩店 *gǔdǒng diàn/gǔwán diàn*
pharmacy	药店 *yàodiàn*

vegetable market	菜市场 *cài shìchǎng*
fruit shop	水果店 *shuíguǒ diàn*
hardware shop	五金店 *wǔjīn diàn*
clothes shop	服装店 *fúzhuāng diàn*
grocers's shop	杂货店/副食店 *záhuò diàn/fùshí diàn*
optician	眼镜店 *yǎnjìng diàn*
silk shop	丝绸店 *sīchóu diàn*
shoe shop	鞋店 *xié diàn*
tobacconist's	烟草店 *yāncǎo diàn*
toy shop	玩具店 *wánjù diàn*
florist	花店 *huā diàn*
jeweller's	珠宝店 *zhūbǎo diàn*
gift shop	礼品店 *lǐpǐn diàn*
craft shop	工艺美术品商店 *gōngyì měishù pǐn shāngdiàn*
sports shop	体育用品商店 *tǐyù yòngpǐn shāngdiàn*
photographic shop	照相器材门市部 *zhàoxiàng qìcái ménshìbù*
newsagent's	报刊门市部 *bàokān ménshìbù*
Is there a ... nearby?	附近有 ... 店吗？ *Fùjìn yǒu ... diàn ma?*

At the bookshop

Do you have ...?

... any English (books/magazines)	英文 (书/杂志) ... *yīngwén (shū/zázhì)*
... a Chinese (textbook/picture book)	中文 (课本/画报) ... *zhōngwén (kèběn/huàbào)*
... an English-Chinese dictionary	英汉字典 ... *yīnghàn zìdiǎn*
... a Chinese-English dictionary	汉英字典 ... *hànyīng zìdiǎn*
... a guide (map/book)	导游 (画/册) ... *dǎoyóu (tú/cè)*
... children's books	儿童书 ... *értóng shū*
... a postcard	明信片 ... *míngxìn piàn*

Is there a cassette to go with this book?	这本课本有录音带吗？ *Zhèiběn kèběn yǒu lùyīndài ma?*
I'd like a book about ...	我想买一本有关 ... 的书 *Wó xiǎng mǎi yìběn yǒuguān ... de shū*
... calligraphy	书法 ... *shūfǎ ...*
... acupuncture	针灸 ... *zhēnjiǔ ...*
... Chinese cookery	中国烹调 ... *Zhōngguó pēngtiáo ...*
... antiques	古董 ... *gúdǒng ...*

Clothes

● You should put the word 件 *jiàn* before all of the following items.

Chinese suit	中山装
	zhōngshān zhuāng
dress	连衣裙
	liányīqún
cheongsam (Chinese dress)	旗袍
	qípáo
coat	大衣
	dàyī
T-shirt	T恤衫
	tīxùshān
silk night gown	丝绸睡袍
	sīchóu shuìpáo
satin robe	锻子长袍
	duànzi chángpáo
jacket	外套/夹克衫
	wàitào/jiākè shān
raincoat	雨衣
	yǔyī
shirt	衬衣
	chènyī
pullover	（套头）毛衣
	(tàotóu) máoyī
sweater	卫生衣/毛衣
	wèishēngyī/máoyī

● You should put the word 条 *tiáo* before the following items.

tie	领带
	lǐngdài
trousers	裤子
	kùzi

belt	皮带
	pídài
panties	短裤
	duǎnkù
skirt	裙子
	qúnzi
underpants	衬裤
	chènkù
scarf	围巾
	wéijīn

You should put the word 双 *shuāng* before the following items.

(leather) shoes	（皮）鞋
	(pí)xié
slippers	拖鞋
	tuōxié
sandals	凉鞋
	liángxié
gloves	手套
	shǒutào
socks	袜子
	wàzi
stockings	长统袜
	chángtǒngwà

The following items can be used as they appear here.

handkerchief	手绢
	shǒujuànr
a suit	一套套装
	yítào tàozhuāng
a pair of pyjamas	一套睡衣
	yítào shuìyī
cap/hat	一顶帽子
	yìdǐng màozi

a bra	一个乳罩 *yíge rǔzhào*
This fits (does not fit) me	这件衣服 (不) 合我身 *Zhèijiàn yīfu (bù) hé wǒ shēn*
Can I try these shoes on?	我试试这双鞋行吗？ *Wǒ shìshi zhèishuāngxié xíng ma?*

It's too ...	太 *tài ...*

... loose	肥 *... féi*
... tight	瘦 *... shòu*
... long	长 *... cháng*
... short	短 *... duǎn*
... big	大 *... dà*
... small	小 *... xiǎo*

Do you have it in (blue)?	有 (蓝色的) 吗？ *Yǒu (lánsède) ma?*
Do you have it with (short/long) sleeves?	有 (短/长) 袖的吗？ *Yǒu (duǎn/cháng) xiùde ma?*
Large (medium/small) size	大 (中/小) 号 *Dà (zhōng/xiǎo) hào*
The zip is broken	拉锁坏了 *Lāsuǒr huàile*
The shoelaces are missing	没有鞋带 *Méiyǒu xiédài*

● For colours see page 136.

Antiques

● All antiques should have a red wax seal. You cannot take them out of China without this seal.

vase	花瓶 *huāpíng*
painting	画 *huà*
pottery/ceramics	陶器 *táoqì*
china/porcelain	瓷器 *cíqì*
dog	狗 *gǒu*
horse	马 *mǎ*
camel	骆驼 *luòtuo*
bamboo chair	竹椅 *zhúyǐ*
screen	屏风 *píngfēng*
fan	扇子 *shànzi*
box	盒子 *hézi*
clock	钟 *zhōng*
watch	表 *biǎo*
rug/carpet	地毯 *dìtǎn*
How old is it?/Which dynasty does it come from?	这是哪个年代的？ *Zhè shì nǎge niándài de?*

Is the export seal on it?

有准许出国的火漆印吗？

Yǒu zhúnxǔ chūguó de huǒqī yìn ma?

Can't you make it any cheaper?

便宜些行吗？

Piányi xiē xíng ma?

You may hear:

清朝的

Qīngcháo de

It's from the Qing Dynasty

一百多年

Yìbǎi duō nián

It's over a hundred years old

我们可以盖

Wǒmén kéyǐ gài

We can put the export seal on for you

对不起，不行

Duì bù qǐ, bùxíng

Sorry, we can't reduce the price

Arts and Crafts

crafts	工艺品
	gōngyìpǐn
ivory carving	牙雕
	yádiāo
wood carving	木雕
	mùdiāo
jade carving	玉雕
	yùdiāo
stone carving	石雕
	shídiāo
agate	玛瑙雕
	mánǎodiāo
glassware	玻璃制品
	bōli zhìpǐn
bamboo toys	竹制玩具
	zhú zhì wánjù

paintings on bamboo/ bamboo scrolls	竹帘画 *zhúlián huà*
shell picture	贝雕画 *bèidiāo huà*
papercuts	剪纸 *jiǎnzhǐ*
kite	风筝 *fēngzhēng*
painted eggshell	彩蛋 *cǎidàn*
lacquer goods	漆具 *qījù*
straw hat	草帽 *cǎomào*
willow basket	柳条篮子 *liǔtiáo lánzi*
filigree work	金丝制品 *jīnsī zhìpǐn*
embroidery	绣花制品 *xiùhūa zhìpǐn*
cloisonne/enamel work	景泰蓝 *jǐngtàilán*
Please could you wrap them for me?	请给我包起来 *Qǐng géi wǒ bāo qǐ lái*

Photographic Supplies

(colour/black and white) film	(彩色/黑白) 胶卷 *(cǎisè/hēibái) jiāojuǎnr*
Japanese (Chinese/American) film	日本 (中国/美国) 胶卷 *rìběn (zhōngguó/měiguó) jiāojuǎnr*
negative	底片 *dǐpiàn*

prints	相片
	xiàngpiàn
slides	幻灯片
	huàndēng piàn
(glossy/matt) finish	(光面/布纹) 纸
	(guāngmiàn/bùwén) zhǐ
When can I pick up the photos?	什么时候来取照片?
	Shénme shíhou láiqù zhàopiàn?

Can you ...?	你能
	Nǐ néng ...
... develop the film	冲卷
	... chōng juǎnr
... enlarge this print	放大洗相
	... fàng dà xǐxiàng
... repair my camera	修相机
	... xiū xiàng jī

The battery isn't working in my camera	相机电池没电了
	Xiàngjī diànchí méi diànle
The film is jammed	胶卷卡住了
	Jiāojuǎn kǎ zhù le
Please could you get it out for me	请给我取出来
	Qǐng géi wǒ qǔ chūlái

Toiletries

comb	梳子
	shūzi
mirror	镜子
	jìngzi
soap	肥皂
	féizào

shampoo	洗发剂
	xǐfàjì
cream	雪花膏
	xuěhuā gāo
perfume	香水
	xiāngshuǐ
lipstick	口红
	kǒuhóng
eye shadow	眼影膏
	yǎnyǐnggāo
nail varnish	指甲油
	zhǐjia yóu
nail clippers	指甲刀
	zhǐjiadāo
toothpaste	牙膏
	yágāo
toothbrush	牙刷
	yáshuā
razor	刮胡刀
	guāhúdāo
razor blade	刀片
	dāopiàn
shaver	电动剃刀
	diàndòng tìdāo
deodorant	除臭剂
	chúchòu jì
sanitary towels	妇女卫生巾
	fùnǚ wèishēng jīn
towel	毛巾
	máojīn
toilet paper	卫生纸
	wèishēng zhǐ

● You should take your own toiletries and medicines to China if possible, as you will probably not be able to get your usual brand there, although Chinese products are of perfectly good quality.

- Note that you should not drink water from the tap. Boiled water is usually provided in hotel rooms for drinking etc.

Tobacco

tobacco	烟 *yān*
filtered cigarettes	过滤嘴烟 *guòlǜzuǐ yān*
a pack of cigarettes	一 (盒/包) 烟 *yì (hé/bāo) yān*
two cartons of cigarettes	两条烟 *liǎng tiáo yān*
a box of matches	一盒火柴 *yì hé huǒchái*
a cigarette lighter	一个打火机 *yíge dáhuǒ jī*
Would you like a cigarette?	请抽支烟 *Qǐng chōu zhī yān*
Thank you, but I don't smoke	我不抽烟，谢谢 *Wǒ bù chōuyān, xièxie*

Beverages

a bottle of ...	一瓶 *yìpíng ...*
... Maotai wine	茅台酒 *... máotái jiǔ*
... ginseng wine	人参酒 *... rénshēnjiǔ*
orange juice	桔子水 *júzi shuǐ*

mineral water	矿泉水
	kuàngquán shuǐ
tea	茶水
	chá shuǐ
black tea	红茶
	hóng chá
green tea	绿茶
	lǜ chá
jasmine tea	茉莉花茶
	mòlihuā chá

Stationery

pen	钢笔
	gāngbǐ
pencil	铅笔
	qiānbǐ
ball-point pen	圆珠笔
	yuánzhūbǐ
eraser	橡皮
	xiàngpí
ruler	格尺
	géchǐ
refill	笔芯
	bǐxīn
envelope	信封
	xìnfēng
writing paper	信纸
	xìnzhǐ
ink	墨水
	mòshuǐ
glue	胶水
	jiāoshuǐ
sticky tape	透明胶带
	tòumíng jiāodài

Jewellery

bracelet	手镯
	shǒuzhuó
brooch	胸针
	xiōngzhēn
earrings	耳环
	ěrhuán
necklace	项链
	xiàngliàn
ring	戒指
	jièzhi
ruby	红宝石
	hóngbǎoshí
sapphire	蓝宝石
	lánbǎoshí
emerald	绿宝石/翡翠
	lǜbǎoshí/fěicuì
turquoise	绿松石
	lǜsōngshí
jade	玉
	yù
ivory	象牙
	xiàng yá
amber	琥珀
	hǔpò
pearl	珍珠
	zhēnzhū
diamond	钻石
	zuànshí
onyx	玛瑙
	mánǎo
amethyst	紫晶
	zǐjīng
gold	金
	jīn

silver	银 *yín*
platinum	白金 *báijīn*
crystal	水晶 *shuǐjīng*
Is it solid gold or gold-plated?	这是纯金还是镀金？ *Zhè shì chúnjīn háishì dùjīn?*
What kind of stone is it?	这是什么宝石？ *Zhè shì shénme bǎoshí?*
I'm sorry, it's too expensive for me	太贵了，买不起 *Tài guì le, mǎibùqǐ*

Tableware

chopsticks	筷子 *kuàizi*
bowl	碗 *wǎn*
cup	杯子 *bēizi*
plate	盘子 *pánzi*
dish	碟子 *diézi*
wok	大勺 *dàsháo*
ladle	勺子 *sháozi*
pot	锅 *guō*
pan	平底锅 *píngdǐguō*
tablecloth	一块桌布 *yíkuài zhuōbù*

At the Post Office

- Most large hotels in China have postal counters
which offer most services for their guests. Opening
hours, however, are often erratic, and you should
look for the sign which indicates when the service is
available (see page 115). Outside the hotel, post
offices are always easy to find, but as a general rule,
main post offices are not usually further apart than,
say, two or three bus stops, and are recognisable by
the green post box outside and sign 邮局. It is
important to remember that, while you can quite
easily post a letter or parcel or make a phone call, it is
not always possible to send international telegrams
from post offices, and you should go to a special
Telegram Building.

Where is the post office?	邮局在哪里？ *Yóu jú zài nǎli?*
Where is the post box (mail box?)	哪儿有邮筒？ *Nǎr yǒu yóutǒng?*

I want to send ... abroad	我要往国外寄 ... *Wǒ yào wǎng guówài jì ...*
... a letter	信 *... xìn*
... a package	包裹 *... bāoguǒ*
... a postcard	明信片 *... míngxìn piàn*

How much is a (stamp)?	(邮票) 多少钱？ *(Yóu piào) duōshao qián?*
airmail letter	航空信 *hángkōng xìn*
express delivery letter	快信 *kuài xìn*
insured letter	保价信 *bǎojià xìn*
registered letter	挂号信 *guàhào xìn*
first class	头等信件 *tóuděng xìnjiàn*
I've come for my package	我来取包裹 *Wǒ lái qǔ bāoguǒ*
Here is my parcel form	这是我的包裹单 *Zhèshì wǒde bāoguǒ dān*
I want to buy four l-yuan-and-6-jiao stamps	我买四张一元六角的邮票 *Wó mǎi sìzhāng yì yuán liù jiǎode yóupiào*

You may see:

办公时间	opening hours
上午	mornings
下午	afternoons
点	... hours
分	... minutes
9点	9 o'clock
11点30分	11.30

Where can I send a ...?	哪里能发 ... ? *Nǎli néng fā ...?*
... telegram/cable	电报/电挂 *... diàn bào/diàn guà*
... fax	传真 *... chuán zhēn*
... telex	电传 *... diàn chuán*
to London/Britain	伦敦/英国 *lúndūn/yīngguó*
Have I filled in the form correctly?	这样写对吗? *Zhè yàng xiě duì ma?*

You may hear:

请填电报单 *Qǐng tián diàn bào dán*	**Please fill in this telegraph form**
对 *duì*	**Yes (you have filled in the form correctly)**
不对 *bù duì*	**No (you have not filled the form in correctly)**
没有头等信件业务 *Méi yǒu tóuděng xìnjiàn yèwù*	**Sorry, we do not have a first-class service**

What is the cost per word?	每个字多少钱? *měige zì duōshao qián?*

Telephoning

Making a phone call in China can be a very frustrating experience, especially if you are trying to make a local call. Surprisingly, international calls are often much easier, possibly because they are placed by the operator; it is not possible to dial them direct from some cities.

I want to make a ...	我要打一个 *Wǒ yào dǎ yíge ...*
... local call	本市电话 *... běnshì diànhuà*
... long-distance call	长途电话 *... chángtú diànhuà*
... international call	国际电话 *... guójì diàn huà*
Can I dial direct?	能直拨吗？ *Néng zhí bō ma?*
How do I get the operator?	怎么找 (接线生/话务员)？ *Zěnme zhǎo (jiēxiàn shēng/huàwù yuán)?*
Operator, please connect me with ...	接綫生，请接 *Jiēxiàn shēng, qǐngjiē ...*
... Dublin	都柏林 *... Dūbólín*
... Edinburgh	爱丁堡 *... Àidīngbǎo*
... New York	纽约 *... Niǔyuē*

The number is 724561

电话 724561
Diànhuà qī èr sì wǔ liù yāo

Please could I talk to Mr Smith?

麻烦您找史密斯先生接电话
Máfan nín zhǎo Smith Xiānshēng jiē diànhuà

I am ...

我就是
Wǒ jiù shì ...

Who's speaking?

您是哪一位？
Nín shì nǎ yí wèi?

Please speak more loudly

请大点声
Qǐng dà diǎn shēng

Please speak slowly

请慢点说
Qǐng màn diǎn shuō

The line is always engaged

总占线
Zǒng zhàn xiàn

I've been cut off

我的电话断了
Wǒde diànhuà duànle

I want to leave a message for Mr Li

请给李先生传个信
Qǐng géi Lǐ xiānsheng chuán ge xìn

It's a wrong number

电话号码不对
Diànhuà hàomǎ búduì

Hold on, please

别挂上，等一下
Bié guà shàng, děng yíxià

There's no answer

没人接电话
Méirén jiē diànhuà

Please cancel the call I booked just now

请取消刚才登记的电话
Qǐng qǔxiāo gāngcái dēngjì de diànhuà

Extension 332, please

请接分机 332
Qǐng jiē fēnjī sān sān èr

I'd like to reverse the charges (make a collect call)

我想请对方付钱
Wó xiǎng qǐng duìfāng fùqián

How much is the call?

我该付多少电话费？
Wǒ gāi fù duōshao diànhuà fèi?

At the bank

- Chinese currency is called *Rénmínbì* (often abbreviated to RMB, meaning literally 'The People's money'). It is divided into *yuán* (usually called *kuài*), *jiǎo* (also known as *máo*) and *fēn* as follows:

  1 *yuán* (kuai) = 10 *jiǎo* = 100 *fēn*

  Chinese notes and coins use our numbering system, so they are easily recognisable. They come in denominations of 100, 50, 10, 5 and 1 *yuán* notes and various smaller denomination notes and coins. Exchange rates are uniform throughout the country, so it is not worth shopping around.

- You will also come across *wàihuìjuàn* or Foreign Exchange Certificates (FEC) which are also divided into *yuán*, *jiǎo* and *fēn*. These have the advantage of being available exclusively to foreigners, and are the only form of currency accepted in the Friendship Stores (and some other places which cater mainly for foreigners). However, you may find that they are not accepted in smaller towns, so it is wise to carry both RMB and FEC if you are planning to travel around.

- Money and traveller's cheques can be exchanged at banks, hotels, Friendship Stores and authorised exchange bureaux. It is important that you keep all your receipts from exchange transactions, as you may not import or export local currency (RMB), and you may be asked for these receipts at customs when you leave. FEC may be exported, but it is probably best to convert them into foreign currency before leaving the country.

- Credit cards are becoming more widely accepted in China, especially in the major cities and tourist areas. It is best, however, to carry either RMB or FEC, just in case.

- As in many countries, there is a black market for currency exchange, and you may be approached in the street and asked *Huàn qián ma?* (Do you exchange money?). You are strongly advised not to deal like this, as it is illegal, and you are likely to get into trouble as result (it is also highly likely that you will lose out on the deal, unless you are very familiar with both language and currency).

I'd like to exchange ...	我要换 *Wǒ yào huàn ...*
... US dollars	美元 *... měiyuán*
... British pounds	英镑 *... yīngbàng*
... Hong Kong dollars	港币 *... gǎngbì*
... Foreign Exchange Certificates	外汇卷 *... wàihuìjuàn*
I'd like to pay by ...	我用 *Wǒ yòng ...*
... cash	现款 *... xiànkuǎn*
... traveller's cheque	旅行支票 *... lǚxíng zhīpiào*
... credit card	信用卡 *... xìnyòng kǎ*
Please give me ...	请给我些 *Qǐng géi wǒ xiē ...*
... large notes	大票 *... dàpiào*
... small notes	小票 *... xiǎopiào*
... coins	硬币 *... yìngbì*
What is the exchange rate?	兑换率是多少？ *Duìhuàn lǜ shì duōshao?*

You may hear:

请看揭示板
Qǐng kàn jiēshì bǎn

Please look at the board

请填表
Qǐng tiánbiǎo

Please fill in this form

请在背面签名
Qǐng zài bèimiàn qiānmíng

Please endorse it

在出纳柜台，那儿
Zài chūnà guìtái nàr

Please go to the cash desk, over there

Where do I cash the cheque?

在哪兑现？
Zài nǎ duìxiàn?

Have you received my transfer?

我的电报转账到了吗？
Wǒde diànbào zhuǎnzhàng dào le ma?

What time do you open/close?

什么时候开门/关门？
Shénme shíhou kāimén/guānmén?

Do you exchange money?

换钱吗？
Huàn qián ma?

Yes (I exchange money)

换
Huàn

No (I don't exchange money)

不换
Bú huàn

Can I use my credit card to withdraw money?

我可以用信用卡取钱吗？
Wǒ kéyǐ yòng xìnyòngkǎ qǔ qián ma?

Here is my passport

这是我的护照
Zhèshì wǒde hùzhào

Can I have a receipt?

能给我一张收据吗？
Néng gěi wǒ yìzhāng shōujù ma?

Can I sign in English?

我可以用英语签名吗？
Wǒ kéyǐ yòng yīngyǔ qiānmíng ma?

Emergencies

● In China, flood and fire are considered the two disasters that should be avoided at all costs, and there are strict penalties imposed on those whose actions have been the cause of such incidents, so beware of leaving cigarettes, running taps etc unattended. If you are unfortunate enough to be caught in a fire, try to call for help: your floor monitor, if you are in your hotel, or the fire brigade. Chinese people will usually rescue foreigners first, so you should find that help comes quickly.

There is a fire	这里着火了 *Zhèli zháohuǒ le*
Where's the fire extinguisher?	哪里有灭火器？ *Náli yǒu mièhuǒ qì?*
Quick, get out!	快从这里跑 *Kuài cóng zhèli pǎo!*

Although as a rule the Chinese are extremely honest, the growth of tourism has inevitably involved an increase in petty crimes, especially theft of foreign currency. Always be sure to lock your door when you leave, and watch out for your wallet or handbag when you are out. If you are unlucky enough to have something stolen, report it immediately to the hotel security official or directly to the police.

I've lost my ...	我的 ... 丢了 *Wǒde ... diūle*
... money	钱 ... *qián* ...
... passport	护照 ... *hùzhào*
... bag	包 ... *bāo* ...
... wallet	钱包 ... *qiánbāo* ...

Please call ...	请叫 ... 来 *Qǐng jiào ... lái*
... the police	警察 *... jǐngchá ...*
... the manager	经理 *... jīnglǐ ...*
Help!	来人哪！ *Lái rén na!*
Stop that man!	抓住那个人！ *Zhuāzhù nèige rén!*
My wallet is missing	我的钱包不见了 *Wǒde qiánbāo bú jiàn le*

You may hear:

What does the ... look like?	你的 ... 什么样？ *Nǐde ... shénme yàng?*
Is this your ...?	你看，这是你的 ... 吗？ *Nǐkàn, zhèshì nǐde ... ma?*

Repairs

● Repair shops are fairly easy to find, and should be able to help with most emergency repairs. Bear in mind, however, that parts for foreign radios, watches etc may not be readily available.

You may see:

修 (理自行) 车	bike repair
修鞋	shoe repair
修表	watch repair
修理眼镜	glasses repair
修锁	lock repair

Can you repair it?	你能修这个吗？ *Nǐ néng xiū zhèige ma?*

When will it be ready?

什么时候能修好？
Shénme shíhou néng xiū hǎo?

You may hear:

什么毛病？
Shénme máobìng?

What's wrong with it?

不能修
Bù néng xiū

It can't be repaired

我能修
Wǒ néng xiū

I can repair it

修好了
Xiū hǎo le

I've repaired it

再找一家修吧
Zài zhǎo yìjiā xiū ba

Try another repair shop

Bicycle repairs

● It goes without saying that where there are a lot of bicycles there are a lot of bicycle repair shops. These can vary from specialist premises to somebody sitting at the roadside with a pump, a basin of water and an assortment of spare parts. Look out for the sign 修车 (*xiūchē*).

I've got a flat tyre

我的车没气了
Wǒ de chē méi qì le.

Could I borrow a pump please?

可以用打气筒吗？
Kéyǐ yòng dǎqì tǒng ma?

Could you repair it as quickly as possible, please?

请快点修好行吗？
Qǐng kuài diǎn xiū hǎo xíng ma?

Shoe repair

● Like bicycle repair shops, shoe repairers can often be found at the roadside surrounded by the tools of their trade.

The heel is broken	鞋跟断了
	Xiégēn duàn le
I'd like these re-heeled with rubber heels	换个鞋胶底跟
	Huàng ge xié jiāodǐ gēn
Please could you change the ...	换
	Huàn ...
... zip	拉锁
	... lāsuǒ
... soles	底
	... dǐ
... heels	跟
	... gēn

Optical repairs

● It is usually fairly easy to get your glasses repaired, but if you wear contact lenses, beware: lenses are still a novelty in large cities and unheard of in many parts of China. Make sure that you take all the necessary cleaning fluids with you and a spare pair of lenses if possible.

The leg of my glasses is broken	我的眼镜腿断了
	Wǒde yǎnjìngtuǐ duàn le
Pleae could you change the lense for me?	换镜片
	Huàn jìng piàn
Can you repair it now?	现在就能修吗?
	Xiànzài jiù néng xiū ma?

You may hear:	
现在就给你修	I'll repair it right now
Xiànzài jiù gěi nǐ xiū	
好了	They're fine now
Hǎo le.	
戴上吧	Try them on
Dàishàng ba	
有毛病你可以再来	Come back if you have any problems
Yǒu máobìng nǐ kéyǐ zàilái	

Watch repair

- China imports a lot of foreign, especially Swiss, watches, so you should be able to find somewhere to carry out at least simple repairs. Look for the sign 修表.

There is something wrong with my watch	我的表出毛病了 *Wǒ de biǎo chū máobìng le*
It's ...	走得 *Zǒu de ...*
... fast	快 *... kuài*
... slow	慢 *... màn*
... stopped	不走了 *... bù zǒu le*
I dropped it	我把它掉地上了 *Wǒ bǎ tā diào dìshàng le*
Can you replace the battery?	你能换电池吗？ *Nǐ néng huàn diànchí ma?*
It was made in ...	是 ... 表 *shì ... biǎo*
Do I need to wait?	我要在这里等吗？ *Wǒ yào zài zhèli děng ma?*

You may hear:	
什么牌子？ *Shénme páizi?*	**What make is it?**
哪国表？ *Nǎ guó biǎo?*	**Where was it made?**
(不)能修 *(Bù) Néng xiū*	**I can (not) repair it**

Laundry

● Most hotels provide a laundry service, but if not, look for the sign 洗衣店 *xǐyīdiàn*.

Please could you ...	请你 *Qǐng nǐ ...*
... dry clean it	干洗 *... gānxǐ*
... iron them	熨好 *... yùn hǎo*
I don't want starch	不上浆 *bú shàng jiāng*
There are (ten) items altogether	一共（十）件 *Yí gòng (shí) jiàn*
When will it be ready?	什么时候能修好？ *Shénme shíhòu néngxiū hǎo?*
I need it this evening	我今晚要用 *Wǒ jīnwǎn yào yòng*

You may hear:	
来取 *... lái qǔ.*	You can collect them ...
明天 *míngtiān ...*	... tomorrow
后天 *hòutiān ...*	... the day after tomorrow
明天上午九点 *míngtiān shàngwǔ jiǔ diǎn ...*	... tomorrow morning at 9 o'clock
明天下午四点 *míngtiān xiàwǔ sì diǎn ...*	... tomorrow afternoon, at four o'clock

Miscellaneous information

- Electric current in China is 220V. You will probably need an adaptor for the Chinese sockets: these adaptors are available at Friendship Stores, or may be borrowed from the hotel.
- Film developing and printing can be done in one or two days. Look for the sign 洗相 *xǐxiàng* and study the phrases on pages 106 and 107.
- It is a good idea to take toilet paper with you when you travel, as it is usually only provided in big hotels.

Anniversaries and holidays

New Year's Day	1 January
Chinese New Year	first three days of the first month of the lunar calendar
Lantern Festival	fifteenth day of the first month of the lunar calendar
International Working Women's Day	8 March
Labour Day	1 May
Chinese Youth Day	4 May
Children's Day	1 June
Dragon Festival	fifth day of the fifth month of the lunar calendar
Mid-autumn Festival	fifteenth day of the eighth month of the lunar calendar
National Day	1 October

- The government offices, factories, schools and shops do not close during general festivals. During important festivals, most services and recreational centres are open for business, but with a skeleton staff. Foreign tourists are not normally inconvenienced by the festivals.

Mean monthly temperatures in main cities (°C)

	Beijing	Shanghai	Guangzhou	Wuhan
Jan	−4.8	3.5	13.7	2.7
Feb	−2.0	4.9	14.6	5.2
Mar	4.3	8.2	17.9	10.0
Apr	13.3	13.7	21.8	18.2
May	19.9	18.6	25.6	21.1
Jun	24.1	23.4	27.3	26.1
Jul	25.8	28.0	28.3	29.1
Aug	24.5	27.6	28.2	28.4
Sep	19.5	23.5	27.0	23.9
Oct	12.6	17.8	23.7	17.6
Nov	4.0	12.5	19.5	11.4
Dec	−2.5	6.5	15.2	5.5

ESSENTIAL INFORMATION

Numbers

0	零 *líng*	5	五 *wǔ*	10	十 *shí*
1	一 *yī*	6	六 *liù*	11 (10+1)	十一 *shíyī*
2	二 *èr*	7	七 *qī*	12 (10+2)	十二 *shíēr*
3	三 *sān*	8	八 *bā*		
4	四 *sì*	9	九 *jiǔ*		

● The remaining numbers are built up according to this pattern.

20	二十 *èrshí*	60	六十 *liùshí*
21	二十一 *èrshíyī*	70	七十 *qīshí*
30	三十 *sānshí*	80	八十 *bāshí*
40	四十 *sìshí*	90	九十 *jiǔshí*
50	五十 *wǔshí*	100	一百 *yìbǎi*

● With the numbers in the hundreds, each digit must be represented, ie 101 is 一百零一 *yìbǎi líng yī* (100 + 0 + 1), and the number of 'tens' must be clear, so that 110 is 一百一十 *yìbǎi yī shí* and 120 is 一百二十 *yìbǎi èr shí*.

- Note that 2 changes to 两 *liǎng* before 千、万、亿, so that 1000 is 一千 *yìqiān* but 2000 is 两千 *liǎng qiān*.
- The thousands are formed as you would expect up to 10,000, which has a special word of its own: 一万 *yíwàn*. Multiples of 10,000 are therefore considered as multiples of *wàn*, not of thousands, as we do. Thus 100,000 is 十万 *shíwàn* (10 × 10,000).
- It is very easy to turn a cardinal number (1, 2, 3, etc) into an ordinal number (1st, 2nd, 3rd etc): you simply add the prefix 第 *dì* to the number, so 第一 *dìyī* = 1st, 第二 *dìèr* = 2nd and so on.

Fractions and Quantities

a half	一半 *yíbàn*	**half a**	半个 *bàn ge*
a quarter	四分之一 *sì fēn zhī yī*	**three quarters**	四分之三 *sì fēn zhī sān*
two thirds	三分之二 *sān fēn zhī èr*		

Months

January	一月 *yīyuè*	**July**	七月 *qīyuè*
February	二月 *èryuè*	**August**	八月 *bāyuè*
March	三月 *sānyuè*	**September**	九月 *jiǔyuè*
April	四月 *sìyuè*	**October**	十月 *shíyuè*
May	五月 *wǔyuè*	**November**	十一月 *shíyīyuè*
June	六月 *liùyuè*	**December**	十二月 *shíèryuè*

Seasons

spring	春天 *chūn (tiān)*	**summer**	夏天 *xià(tiān)*
autumn/fall	秋天 *qiū (tiān)*	**winter**	冬天 *dōng (tiān)*

Days

Monday	星期一 *xīngqīyī*	**Friday**	星期五 *xīngqīwǔ*
Tuesday	星期二 *xīngqīèr*	**Saturday**	星期六 *xīngqīliù*
Wednesday	星期三 *xīngqīsān*	**Sunday**	星期日/天 *xīngqīrì/tiān*
Thursday	星期四 *xīngqīsì*		

What is the date today?	今天几号 *Jīntiān jǐhào?*
Today is ...	今天 *Jīntiān ...*
this month	这个月 *zhèige yuè*
last month	上个月 *shàngge yuè*
next month	下个月 *xiàge yuè*
every month	每个月 *měige yuè*
two months ago	两个月前 *liǎngge yuè qián*
in two months (time)	两个月后 *liǎngge yuè hòu*
within three months	三个月内 *sānge yuè nèi*

a year ago	一年前 *yìnián qián*
three years ago	大前年 *dà qiánnián*
the year before last	前年 *qiánnián*
last year	去年 *qùnián*
this year	今年 *jīnnián*
next year	明年 *míngnián*
the year after next	后年 *hòunián*
last week	上星期 *shàng xīngqī*
next week	下星期 *xià xīngqī*
the day before yesterday	前天 *qiántiān*
yesterday	昨天 *zuótiān*
today	今天 *jīntiān*
tomorrow	明天 *míngtiān*
the day after tomorrow	后天 *hòutiān*
before the weeked	周末前 *zhōumò qián*
holiday	假日 *jiàrì*
morning	上午 *shàngwǔ*

afternoon	下午
	xiàwǔ
evening	晚上
	wǎnshàng
noon	中午
	zhōngwǔ
midnight	夜里
	yièli

Telling the time

● China is approximately eight hours ahead of Europe.

... o'clock	点
	... diǎn
5 o'clock	五点
	wǔdiǎn
half past ...	点半
	... diǎn bàn
half past three	三点半
	sāndiǎn bàn
five past ...	点五分
	... diǎn wǔ fēn
ten past ...	点十分
	... diǎn shí fēn
quarter past ...	点十五分
	... diǎn shí wǔ fēn
twenty past ...	点二十分
	... diǎn èr shí fēn
twenty five past ...	点二十五分
	... diǎn èr shí wǔ fēn
twenty five to ...	点三十五分
	... diǎn sān shí wǔ fēn
twenty to ...	点四十分
	... diǎn sì shí fēn
quarter to ...	点四十五分
	... diǎn sì shí wǔ fēn

ten to ...	点五十分 *... diǎn wǔ shí fēn*
five to ...	点五十五分 *... diǎn wǔ shí wǔ fēn*
What's the time?	几点了 *jí diǎn le?*
twenty minutes early	提前二十分钟 *tíqián èrshí fēnzhōng*
twenty minutes late	晚二十分钟 *wǎn èrshí fēnzhōng*

Weather

● China is a very large country, and has a correspondingly large range of climate. The best time to go is spring or autumn, as the summer months tend to be hot and humid, with a lot of rainfall. You will find, however, that the Chinese do not use the weather as a conversational topic as westerners often do.

It's raining	下雨了 *Xià yǔ le*
It's snowing	下雪了 *Xià xuě le*
It's windy	刮风了 *Guāfēng le*
It's freezing	结冰了 *Jiébīng le*
It's getting dark	天黑了 *Tiān hēi le*
It's late	天晚了 *Tiān wǎn le*
It's very warm	天真暖和 *Tiān zhēn nuǎnhuo*
It's nice and cool	天真凉快 *Tiān zhēn liángkuài*

It's very dry	天真干燥
	Tiān zhēn gānzào
It's very damp	天真潮湿
	Tiān zhēn cháoshī
What a strong wind!	风真大！
	Fēng zhēn dà!
What a downpour!	雨真大！
	Yǔ zhēn dà!
It's terribly hot	热死了！
	Rè sǐ le
It's terribly cold	冷死了！
	Lěng sǐ le

Directions

front	前
	qián
back	后
	hòu
left	左
	zuǒ
right	右
	yòu
in front of ...	在 ... 前面
	zài ... qián miàn
behind ...	在 ... 后面
	zài ... hòumiàn
to the left of ...	在 ... 左面
	zài ... zuǒmiàn
to the right of ...	在 ... 右面
	zài ... yòumiàn

east	东	south	南
	dōng		*nán*
west	西	north	北
	xī		*běi*

135

Colours

black	黑色 *hēisè*	**blue**	蓝色 *lánsè*
yellow	黄色 *huángsè*	**white**	白色 *báisè*
red	红色 *hóngsè*	**green**	绿色 *lǜsè*
pink	粉色 *fěnsè*	**purple**	紫色 *zǐsè*
orange	桔红色 *júhóngsè*	**brown**	褐色 *hèsè*
light	浅色 *qiǎnsè*	**dark**	深色 *shēnsè*

Important signs

Gentlemen	男厕所 *nán cèsuǒ*
Ladies	女厕所 *nǚ cèsuǒ*
Vacant	无人/空 *wúrén/kōng*
Occupied	有人/占用 *yǒurén/zhànyòng*
Pull	拉 *lā*
Push	推 *tuī*
Open/on	开 *kāi*
Close/off	关 *guān*
Exit	出口 *chū kǒu*
Entrance	入口 *rù kǒu*

Emergency Exit	太平门 *tàipíng mén*
Danger	危险 *wēixiǎn*
Cold	冷 *lěng*
Hot	热 *rè*
Not drinking water	非饮用水 *fēi yǐnyòng shuǐ*
No smoking	禁止吸烟 *jìnzhǐ xīyān*
No photos allowed	禁止拍照/摄影 *jìnzhǐ pāizhào/shēyǐng*
No litter	禁止扔废纸 *jìnzhǐ rēng fèizhǐ*
No entry	禁止入内 *jìnzhǐ rùnèi*
Staff only	闲人免入 *xiánrén miǎnrù*
Please do not touch	勿动/摸 *wù dòng/mō*
Waiting room	候车室 *hòuchē shì*
Information desk	问事处 *wèn shì chù*
Booking office	售票处 *shòupiào chù*
Lift (elevator)	电梯 *diàntī*
Caution	小心 *xiǎoxīn*
Sold out	售完 *shòuwán*
Cash desk	出纳 *chūnà*

Please do not disturb	请勿打扰 *Qǐng wù dǎrǎo*
No parking	禁止停车 *jìnzhǐ tíng chē*
Lost property office	失物招领处 *shīwù zhāolǐng chù*
Exchange bureau	外币兑换 *wàibì duìhuàn*
Admission free	免费入场 *miǎnfèi rùchǎng*
Admission by ticket only	凭票入场 *píngpiào rùchǎng*
No swimming	禁止游泳 *jìnzhǐ yóuyǒng*
Customs	海关 *hǎiguān*
Friendship Store	友谊商店 *yǒuyì shāngdiàn*
fitting room	试衣室 *shìyīshì*
bank	银行 *yínháng*
taxi	出租车 *chūzūchē*
toilet	厕所 *cèsuǒ*
Keep off the grass	勿踏草地 *Wù tà cǎodì*
Business hours	营业时间 *Yíngyè shíjiān*
cinema	电影院 *diànyǐng yuàn*
theatre	剧院/场 *jùyuàn/chǎng*

WORDLIST

A

a/an yī 一

to be able to néng 能, kéyǐ 可以

about dàyuē 大约, guānyú 关于

above zài shàngmiàn 在上面, dàyú 大于

abroad guówài 国外

account zhàngdān 帐单,

ache téng 疼, tòng 痛
  headache tóutòng 头痛
  toothache yátòng 牙痛

act zuò 做, bànyǎn 扮演

acting biǎoyǎn 表演

address dìzhǐ 地址

admission yǔnxǔ jìnrù 允许进入

to afford mǎi de qǐ 买得起

afraid kǒngpà 恐怕

after zài hòumiàn 在后面, hòulái 后来

afternoon xiàwǔ 下午

again zài 在, yòu 又

age niánlíng 年令

agency shè 社
  travel agency lǚxíngshè 旅行社

ahead zài ... zhīqián 在 ... 之前

aircraft fēijī 飞机

airmail hángkōng xìn 航空信

airport (fēi) jīchǎng (飞)机场

airport waiting room hòujīshì 候机室

alcohol jiǔ 酒

all quántǐ 全体, dōu 都
  all at once yíxià 一下
  all right hǎo 好, xíng 行
  not at all méi shénme 没什么, méiguānxi 没关系

allergy guòmǐn 过敏

already yǐjīng 已经

also yě 也, hái 还

always zǒngshì 总是

a.m. shàngwǔ 上午

am shì 是

ambassador dàshǐ 大使

amber hǔpò 琥珀

ambulance jiùhù chē 救护车

America Měiguó 美国

American Měiguó rén 美国人

amusing dòulè de 逗乐的, hǎowánr 好玩儿

and hé 和, yú 与

aniseed dàliào 大料

another zài yíge 再一个, lìng yíge 另一个

antidiarrhoeal zhǐxiè yào 止泻药

antique shop gǔdǒng diàn 古董店, gǔwán diàn 古玩店

anxious jiāojí de 焦急的

appearance yàngzi 样子

apple píngguǒ 苹果

to apply shēnqǐng 申请, shìyòng 适用

April sìyuè 四月

apron wéiqún 围裙

are shì 是

aren't búshì 不是

arm gēbo 胳膊

around dàyuē 大约

to arrange ānpái 安排

to arrive dào (dá) 到(达)

art měishù 美术, yìshù 艺术

ash huī 灰
  ash tray yānhuī dié / gāng 烟灰碟/缸

to ask wèn 问
  to ask for yào 要

aspirin āsīpǐlín 阿司匹林

assemble jíhé 集合

at zài 在

athlete yùndòng yuán 运动员

athletics yùndòng 运动

atlas dìtú cè 地图册

attendant fúwù yuán 服务员
attention zhùyì 注意
August bāyuè 八月
Australia Àodàlìyà 澳大利亚
autumn qiūtiān/jì 秋天/季
awful hěn 很

B

back (direction) xiànghòu
 向后, **(body)** hòubù 后部,
 bèi 背
 at the back hòumiàn 后面
bad huài 坏, chòu 臭, bùhǎo
 不好
bag bāo 包, dàizi 袋子
baggage xíngli 行李
balcony yángtái 阳台
ball qiú 球
 ball game qiúsài 球赛
ballet bālěiwǔ 芭蕾舞
ballpoint pen yuánzhū bǐ
 圆珠笔
bamboo zhúzi 竹子
banana xiāngjiāo 香蕉
band dàizi 带子
bank yínháng 银行
 bank note chāopiào 钞票
banquet yànhuì 宴会
barber lǐfà shī 理发师
 barber's lǐfà guǎn 理发馆
basket lánzi 篮子
 basket-ball lánqiú 篮球
bath xǐzǎo 洗澡
to bathe xǐ 洗
bathroom yùshì 浴室
battery diànchí 电池
bazaar shìchǎng 市场
to be shì 是
bean dòu 豆
beancurd dòufu 豆腐
bean sprouts dòuyá 豆芽
beard húxū 胡须
to beat yíng 赢
beautiful měi (lì) de 美(丽)的
beauty měi 美
 beauty parlour měiróng
 yuàn 美容院
because yīnwèi 因为
bed chuáng 床
bed-clothes chuángshàng
 yòngpǐn 床上用品

bedroom wòshì 卧室
beef niúròu 牛肉
beer píjiǔ 啤酒
before yǐqián 以前, zài ...
 yǐqián 在 ... 以前
 before long bùjiǔ 不久
to begin kāishǐ 开始
behind zàihòumiàn 在后面,
 zai ... hòumiàn 在 ... 后面
bell zhōng 钟, líng 铃
belly dùzi 肚子
below zài ... xià 在 ... 下
 below zero líng (dù yǐ) xià
 零(度以)下
belt yāodài 腰带
to bend wān (yāo) 弯(腰)
berth wòpù 卧铺
best zuìhǎo de 最好的
better hǎo 好, gèng hǎo
 更好
bicycle zìxíngchē 自行车
big dà (de) 大(的)
bill zhàng dān 帐单
 to pay a bill fùzhàng 付帐
birthday shēngrì 生日
bit yìdiǎn 一点
 a bit yǒu diǎnr 有点儿,
 yī diǎnr 一点儿
bitter kǔ 苦
black hēi (sè) 黑(色)
blanket tǎnzi 毯子
to bleed liúxuè 流血
block zǔsè 阻塞
 to block up dǔle 堵了
blood xuè 血
blouse nǚchènshān 女衬衫
to blow guāfēng 刮风, chuī 吹
blue lán (sè) 蓝(色)
board bǎn 板
boat chuán 船
body shēntǐ 身体
bone gútou 骨头
book shū 书
 bookshop shūdiàn 书店
to book yùdìng 预订/定
 book seats/tickets dìngpiào
 订票
 booking office shòupiào
 chù 售票处
to borrow jiè 借
both liǎng 两, dōu 都
bottle píngzi 瓶子

bowl wǎn 碗
box xiāngzi 箱子, hézi 盒子
box-office shòupiào chù 售票处
boy nánhái 男孩, xiǎohuǒzi 小伙子
bra rǔzhào 乳罩
bracelet shǒuzhuó 手镯
brandy báilándì 白兰地
bread miànbāo 面包
to break dǎhuài 打坏, chū máobìng 出毛病
breakfast zǎofàn 早饭
breast xiōngbù 胸部
breath hūxī 呼吸
to breathe hūxī 呼吸
bright míngliàng 明亮
to bring nálái 拿来
Britain Yīngguó 英国
British Yīngguó rén 英国人
broken huài le 坏了
brooch xiōngzhēn 胸针
brother xiōngdì 兄弟
brush shuāzi 刷子
buffet zìzhùcān (guìtái) 自助餐 (柜台)
building jiànzhù wù 建筑物, dàlóu 大楼
bulb dēngpào 灯泡
to burn shāo 烧
bus gōnggòng qìchē 公共汽车
  bus stop / station qìchē zhàn 汽车站
business yíngyè 营业
  business hours yíngyè shíjiān 营业时间
  businessman shāngrén 商人
busy máng 忙, zhànxiàn 占线
but dànshì 但是, chúle 除了
butter huángyóu 黄油
to buy mǎi 买

C

cabbage juǎnxīn cài 卷心菜
  Chinese cabbage / leaves báicài 白菜
cabin chuáncān 船舱

cable (hǎidǐ) diànbào (海底) 电报, diànguà 电挂
cake dàngāo 蛋糕, bǐng 饼
to calculate jìsuàn 计算
calendar rìlì 日历
to call jiào 叫, dǎ diànhuà 打电话, chēnghū 称呼
camel luòtuo 骆驼
camera zhàoxiàng jī 照相机
can huì 会, néng 能, kěyǐ 可以
  can't afford mǎi bùqǐ 买不起
Canada Jiānádà 加拿大
to cancel qǔxiāo 取消
candy tángguǒ 糖果
Canton Guǎngzhōu 广州
cap màozi 帽子
capital shǒudū 首都
car xiǎo qìchē 小汽车
  car-sick yūnchē 晕车
card kǎpiàn 卡片
to care xiǎoxīn 小心
  to take care xiǎoxīn 小心
careful xiǎoxīn de 小心的, zǐxì de 仔细的
carpet dìtǎn 地毯, máotǎn 毛毯
carrot húluóbo 胡萝卜
to carry bān 搬
case hézi 盒子
cash xiànjīn 现金
to cash duìxiàn 兑现
cashier chūnà 出纳
cat māo 猫
to catch zhuāzhù 抓住
cauliflower càihuā 菜花
cave dòng 洞
celery qíncài 芹菜
central heating nuǎnqì 暖气
centre zhōngxīn 中心, zhōngjiān 中间
certainly dāngrán 当然
certificate zhèngmíng 证明
chair yǐzi 椅子
chairman zhǔxí 主席
champagne xiāngbīn jiǔ 香槟酒
to change duìhuàn 兑换, huàn 换
  change língqián 零钱
  to give change zhǎoqián 找钱

small change língqián
零钱
character zì 字
charge shōufèi 收费, jiàqián
价钱
chart tú(biǎo) 图(表)
cheap piányi 便宜
check jiǎnchá 检查
to check in dēngjì 登记
to check in baggage tuōyùn
托运
cheers gānbēi 干杯
chef chúshī 厨师
chemical yàopǐn 药品
cheque (check) zhīpiào 支票
chest xiōng 胸
chicken jī 鸡
child / children háizi 孩子,
értóng 儿童
China Zhōngguó 中国
china cíqì 瓷器
Chinese (person, language)
Zhōngguó rén 中国人,
Zhōngwén 中文, Hànyǔ
(object) 汉语 Zhōngguó de
中国的
Chinese food / meal
zhōngcān 中餐
Chinese tunic suit / Chinese
jacket Zhōngshān
zhuāng 中山装
chopsticks kuàizi 筷子
Christmas Shèngdàn jié
圣诞节
cigarette xiāngyān 香烟
filtered cigarette
guòlǜzuǐyān 过滤嘴烟
cigarette stub yāntóu
烟头
cinema diànyǐng yuàn 电影院
circus mǎxì(tuán) 马戏(团)
city chéngshì 城市
clam géli 蛤蜊
clear míngbai 明白
clinic wèishēng suǒ 卫生所
clock zhōng 钟
to close guānmén 关门
close (near) jìn de 近的
cloth bù 布
clothes yīfu 衣服, fúzhuāng
服装
coat shàngyī 上衣

cocoa kěkě 可可
coffee kāfēi 咖啡
coin yìngbì 硬币
cold lěng 冷, liáng 凉,
gǎnmào 感冒
common cold gǎnmào
感冒
cold dish liángcài 凉菜
college xuéyuàn 学院, dàxué
大学
colour yánsè 颜色
light colour qiǎnsè 浅色
dark colour shēnsè 深色
comb shūzi 梳子
to comb shū 梳
to come lái 来, láidào 来到
to come from chūshēngyú
出生于, láizì 来自
to come in jìnlai 进来
commerce mǎimài 买卖
common pǔtōng de 普通
company gōngsī 公司, péibàn
陪伴
to compare bǐjiào 比较
competition bǐsài 比赛
completely wánquán de
完全的
concert yīnyuè huì 音乐会
condition tiáojiàn 条件
conductor shòupiào yuán
售票员, zhǐhuī 指挥
to connect jiē 接
connection liánxi 联系
consulate lǐngshì guǎn 领事馆
to contact liánxi 联系
contest bǐsài 比赛
cook chúshī 厨师
to cook pēngtiáo 烹调, shāo
烧
cool liáng 凉
pleasantly cool liángkuài
凉快
to cooperate hézuò 合作
copper tóng 铜
copy fùzhì pǐn 复制品, běn
本
to copy chāoxiě 抄写, lù 录
fùzhì 复制
correct duì 对, búcuò 不错,
shì 是
cosmetics huàzhuāng pǐn
化粧品

cost jiàgé 价格, fèiyòng 费用
costume fúzhuāng 服装
cotton mián(de) 棉(的)
cough késou 咳嗽
could néng 能, huì 会, kěyǐ 可以
to count jìsuàn 计算
country guójiā 国家
countryside nóngcūn 农村
couple yīshuāng 一双, fūfù 夫妇
cover zhào 罩
to cover gài 盖
craft gōngyì 工艺
crab pángxiè 螃蟹
cream nǎiyóu 奶油, xuěhuā gāo 雪花膏
credit card xìnyòng kǎ 信用卡
crisp sūde 酥的
to cross guò 过
crossing lùkǒu 路口
crystal shuǐjīng 水晶
cucumber huángguā 黄瓜
cup bēizi 杯子
currency huòbì 货币
curtain chuānglián 窗帘
customs hǎiguān 海关, fēngsú 风俗
to cut jiǎn 剪
  to cut off duàn 断
cycle qí zìxíngchē 骑自行车

D

damp cháoshī de 潮湿的
to dance tiàowǔ 跳舞
  dance wǔdǎo 舞蹈, wǔhuì 舞会
danger / dangerous wēixiǎn 危险
to dare gǎn 敢
dark hēi 黑, àn 暗
date rìqī 日期, hào 号
daughter nǚ'ér 女儿
dawn tiānliàng 天亮
day (yì)tiān (一)天, (yí)rì (一)日, báitiān 白天
  the day after tomorrow hòutiān 后天
  the day before yesterday qiántiān 前天

death sǐ(wáng) 死(亡)
debt qiànzhàng 欠帐
December shí'èr yuè 十二月
degree dù 度, xuéwèi 学位
  degree (of temperature) qìwēn 气温
delay yánwù 延误
to deliver sòng 送
dentist yáyī 牙医
deodorant chúchòujì 除臭剂
department store bǎihuò shāngdiàn 百货商店
deposit yājīn 押金
desk shūzhuō 书桌
to develop a film chōngjuǎn 冲卷
diamond zuànshí 钻石
dictionary zìdiǎn 字典
to die sǐ 死
diet shíwù 食物
difficult nán 难
dining car cānchē 餐车
dining room cāntīng 餐厅
dinner wǎnfàn 晚饭
direct zhíjiē 直接
to disappear bùjiàn 不见
disco dísīkē 迪斯科
disease bìng 病
disgusting ěxin 恶心
dish pánzi 盘子
to dislike bù xǐhuan 不喜欢
dislocation tuōjiù 脱臼
to display biǎoyǎn 表演
to dive tiàoshuǐ 跳水
dizzy tóuyūn 头晕
to do zuò 做, gàn 干
  to do business yíngyè 营业
  don't bié 别, búyào 不要, wù 勿
  don't mention it búyào kèqì 不要客气
doctor yīshēng 医生, dàifu 大夫
documentary film jìlù piān 记录片
dog gǒu 狗
door mén 门
doorway ménkǒu 门口
double shuāngde 双的
  double bed shuāngrén chuáng 双人床

double room shuāngrén fángjiān 双人房间

down xià 下, xiàngxià 向下

downstairs lóuxià 楼下

  to go downstairs xiàlóu 下楼

dragon lóng 龙

drama xì jù 戏剧

to draw / drawing huà 画

dress fúzhuāng 服装

  be dressed in chuānzhúo 穿着

  a woman's dress liányīqún 连衣裙

to dress chuānyī 穿衣

to drink hē 喝, hē shuǐ 喝水

  drink a toast gānbēi 干杯

  drinking water yǐnyòng shuǐ 饮用水

drink jiǔ 酒

to drive kāichē 开车

driver sījī 司机

drizzle xiǎoyǔ 小雨

to drop diào 掉

drug yàowù 药物

drugstore yàodiàn 药店

drum gǔ 鼓

drunk zuì 醉

dry gānzào 干燥

to dry biàngān 变干

to blow dry chuīgān 吹干

Dublin Dūbólín 都柏林

duck yā 鸭

duty zérèn 责任

  on duty zhíbān 值班, zhíqín 值勤

to dye rǎn 染

E

each měige 每个

ear ěrduo 耳朵

early zǎo 早

earrings ěrhuán 耳环

earth dì(qiú) 地(球)

east dōng 东

to eat chī 吃

economy-class pǔtōng 普通

Edinburgh Àidīngbǎo 爱丁堡

egg dàn 蛋

eggplant qiézi 茄子

eight bā 八

eighteen shíbā 十八

eighty bāshí 八十

either yě(bù) 也(不)

elder dàde 大的

  elder brother gēge 哥哥

  elder sister jiějie 姐姐

eldest zuì dàde 最大的

electricity diàn 电

elevator diàntī 电梯

eleven shíyī 十一

else bié de 别的

embassy dàshǐ guǎn 大使馆

to embroider xiùhuā 绣花

emerald fēicuì 翡翠, lǜbǎoshí 绿宝石

emergency exit tàipíngmén 太平门

emergency room jízhěn shì 急诊室

emperor huángdì 皇帝

empty kōng 空

end jìntóu 尽头, zhōngdiǎn 终点

England Yīngguó 英国

English Yīngwén 英文, Yīngyǔ 英语, Yīngguó rén 英国人

to enjoy xǐhuān 喜欢, xīnshǎng 欣赏

enough zúgòu 足够

to enquire about dǎtīng 打听

enquiry office wènxùnchù 问讯

to enter jìn(rù) 进(入)

to entertain / entertainment kuǎndài 款待, zhāodài 招待

entrance ménkǒu 门口, rùkǒu 入口

envelope xìnfēng 信封

equipment qìcái 器材

eraser xiàngpí 橡皮

evening wǎnshàng 晚上

every měige 每个

exactly zhèngshì 正是

to examine jiǎnchá 检查, zhěnchá 诊察

excellent hǎo jí le 好极了, jíhǎo 极好

to exchange (duì) huàn (兑)换

exchange rate duìhuàn lǜ 兑换率
to excuse yuánliàng 原谅
excuse me Duì bù qǐ 对不起,
　　Qǐng yuánliàng 请原谅
　(to get attention) Láojià 劳驾
　(when someone is in your way) Jièguāng 借光
　Excuse me, but could you tell me ... Qǐngwèn ... 请问 ...
exercise yùndòng 运动, liànxí 练习
exhibition zhǎnlǎn huì 展览会
exit chūkǒu 出口, tàipíng mén 太平门
expect qīwàng 期望
expensive guì de 贵的
to explain jiěshì 解释, jiǎng 讲
export chūkǒu 出口
express letter kuàixìn 快信
express train kuàichē 快车
extension (of a telephone) fēnjī 分机
external guówài 国外
Europe Ōuzhōu 欧洲
eye yǎnjīng 眼睛
eyebrow pencil méibǐ 眉笔
eye-drops yǎnyào shuǐ 眼药水
eye-shadow yǎnyǐng gāo 眼影膏

F

face miàn 面, liǎn 脸
factory gōngchǎng 工厂
to fall diào 掉, shuāijiāo 摔交
family jiā 家, jiārén 家人
famous yǒumíng de 有名的
fan shànzi 扇子
far yuǎn (de) 远(的)
fare chēfèi 车费
fashionable liúxíng 流行
fast kuài 快
fat féi 肥, pàng 胖
　fat (for cooking) féiyóu 肥油
fate mìngyùn 命运
father fùqin 父亲

fault máobìng 毛病, cuò 错
feather yǔmáo 羽毛
February èryuè 二月
fee fèiyòng 费用
to feel mō 摸, gǎndào 感到
feet jiǎo 脚
female nǚ 女
festival jiérì 节日
fever fāshāo 发烧
few shǎo 少
　a few yìxiē 一些, jǐge 几个
fifteen shíwǔ 十五
fifth dìwǔ 第五
fifty wǔshí 五十
figure shùzi 数字
to fill tián 填, bǔ 补
film diànyǐng 电影, jiāojuǎnr 胶卷
　film star diànyǐng míngxīng 电影明星
to find zhǎo 找
fine hǎo 好, qíng 晴
fire huǒ 火
　to be on fire / catch fire zháohuǒ 着火
　fire extinguisher mièhuǒ qì 灭火器
first dìyī 第一, kāishǐ 开始
　first aid jíjiù 急救
　first-class tóuděng 头等
fish yú 鱼
to fish diàoyú 钓鱼
fit (healthy) héshēn 合身, jiànkāng 健康
five wǔ 五
flag qí 旗
flat tàojiān 套间
flavour wèi 味
flesh ròu 肉
flight fēi 飞, hángbān 航班
floor lóucéng 楼层
　floor monitor fúwùyuán 服务员
florist huādiàn 花店
flour miànfěn 面粉
flower huā 花
　flower vase huāpíng 花瓶
fluffy péngsōng 蓬松
to fly fēi 飞, chéng fēijī 乘飞机
fog wù 雾
foggy yǒuwù 有雾

to be fond (of) xǐhuan 喜欢,
xǐ'ài 喜爱
food shíwù 食物
foot jiǎo 脚
football zúqiú 足球
for wèile 为了, yīnwei 因为,
xiàng 向
to forbid jìnzhǐ 禁止, bùzhǔn
不准, bùxǔ 不许
foreign wàiguó de 外国的
foreign country wàiguó
外国
foreign exchange wàihuì
外汇, wàibì 外币
**FEC (Foreign Exchange
Certificates)** Wàihuì juàn
外汇卷
to forget wàngjì 忘记
form biǎo (gé) 表(格)
forty sìshí 四十
forward xiàng qián 向前
to forward 向前, zhuǎnjì
转寄
fountain-pen gāngbǐ 钢笔
four sì 四
fourteen shísì 十四
fraction fēnshù 分数
fracture gǔzhé 骨折
free miǎnshuì de 免税的,
bùmáng 不忙
free of charge miǎnfèi
免费
to freeze jiébīng 结冰
French bean càidòu 菜豆
fresh xīnxiān de 新鲜的
Friday xīng qī wǔ 星期五
fried jiān 煎, zhá 炸, chǎo 炒
friend péngyou 朋友
boyfriend nán péngyou
男朋友
girlfriend nǚ péngyou 女朋
友
friendship yǒuyì 友谊
Friendship Store Yǒuyì
Shāngdiàn 友谊商店
fringe liúhǎir 刘海儿
from cóng 从
front qiánmiàn 前面
fruit shuǐguǒ 水果
fruit juice guǒzhī 果汁
full mǎnde 满的
to be full bǎo le 饱了

funny hǎowánr 好玩儿
fur máopí 毛皮

G

game bǐsài 比赛
garlic dàsuàn 大蒜
gate dàmén 大门
to gather jíhé 集合
gentleman xiānsheng 先生
Gentlemen / Gents nán cèsuǒ
男厕所
to get yǒu 有, mǎi 买,
shōudào 收到, dào 到,
biàndé 变得
to get better hǎo xiē le
好些子
to get up qǐchuáng 起床,
qǐlái 起来
to have got to bù dé bù
不得不
gift lǐwù 礼物, lǐpǐn 礼品
ginger jiāng 姜
ginseng rénshēn 人参
girl nǚhái 女孩
to give gěi 给
glad gāoxìng 高兴
glass bōli 玻璃, bōli bēi
玻璃杯
glasses yǎnjìng 眼镜
glove shǒutào 手套
glue jiāoshuǐ 胶水
to go qù 去, wǎng 往, zǒu 走
to go back huíqù 回去
to go into jìnqù 进去
to go out chūqù 出去
to go to dào 到, shàng 上,
qùkàn 去看, qùtīng 去听
gold jīn 金
gold-plating dùjīn 镀金
good hǎo 好, yúkuài de
愉快的
to be good at huì 会
good afternoon xiàwǔ hǎo
下午好
good evening wǎnshàng
hǎo 晚上好, wǎn'ān 晚安
good morning zǎoshàng
hǎo 早上好
good night wǎn'ān
晚安
good-bye zàijiàn 再见

goods shāngpǐn 商品, huòwù 货物
gorge xiá 峡
gown chángpáo 长袍
grape pútao 葡萄
  grape wine pútao jiǔ 葡萄酒
grass cǎo 草
grease yóu 油
greasy yóunì 油腻
great wěidà de 伟大, hěnhǎo de 很好
  the Great Wall Chángchéng 长城
green lǜ(sè) 绿(色)
to greet wènhòu 问候, huānyíng 欢迎
grey (gray) huī(sè) 灰(色)
grocer's shípǐn diàn 食品店, záhuò diàn 杂货店
group xiǎozǔ 小组, tuántǐ 团体
guesthouse bīnguǎn 宾馆, zhāodài suǒ 招待所
guide dǎoyóu 导游
gymnasium tǐyù guǎn 体育馆
gymnastics tǐcāo 体操

H

hair tóufa 头发, máo 毛
haircut lǐfà 理发
hairpin fàqiǎ 发卡
hairdresser lǐfà shī 理发师
  hairdresser's lǐfà guǎn 理发馆
half yíbàn 一半
hall táng 堂, tīng 厅
hand shǒu 手
handbag shǒutí bāo 手提包
handkerchief shǒujuàn 手绢
happy gāoxìng 高兴
hard yìng 硬, nán 难
hardware wǔjīn 五金
has yǒu 有
hat màozi 帽子
to have yǒu 有, chī 吃, hē 喝, gǎnshòu 感受
  to have a meal chīfàn 吃饭
  to have a pleasant journey yílù shùnfēng 一路顺风

to have an attack of one's old illness fànbìng 犯病
to have an injection dǎzhēn 打针
to have diarrhoea xièdù 泻肚
he tā 他
head tóu 头
headache tóutòng 头痛
health jiànkāng 健康
to hear tīngjiàn 听见
heart xīn 心, xīnzàng 心脏
  heart disease xīnzàng bìng 心脏病
heat rè 热
height gāo(dù) 高(度)
hello wèi 喂
to help bāng (máng) 帮(忙)
  Help! Jiùmìng! 救命!
hen's egg jīdàn 鸡蛋
her tā(de) 她(的)
here zhèli 这里, zhèr 这儿
hero yīngxióng 英雄
herself tā zìjǐ 她自己
high gāo 高
hill xiǎoshān 小山
him tā 他
himself tā zìjǐ 他自己
to hire zū 租
his tā de 他的
history lìshǐ 历史
to hit dǎ 打
hobby àihào 好爱
to hold ná 拿, bào 抱, zhuāng 装, bǎ 把
holiday jiérì 节日, jiàrì 假日
home jiā 家
  (adv) huíjiā 回家
  Make yourself at home Búyào kèqi 不要客气
Hong Kong dollar Gǎngbì 港币
honey fēngmì 蜂蜜
to hope xīwàng 希望
horse mǎ 马
hospital yīyuàn 医院
hospitality kuǎndài 款待, zhāodài 招待
host (ná)zhǔrén (男)主人
hostess nǚzhǔrén 女主人
hot rè 热, là 辣
  hot dish rècài 热菜

Wordlist

hotel lǚguǎn 旅馆, lǚshè 旅社, zhāodài suǒ 招待所; fàndiàn 饭店
hour xiǎoshí 小时
hors d'oeuvres lěngpán 冷盘
house fángzi 房子, jiā 家
how zěnyàng 怎样, zěnme 怎么
　How are you? Nǐ hǎo ma? 你好吗?
　How do you do? Nǐ hǎo 你好
　how big/large duōdà 多大
　how long duōcháng 多长
　how much/many duōshao 多少, jǐ 几
hundred bǎi 百
hungry è 饿
to hurry gǎnjǐn 赶紧
husband àiren 爱人, zhàngfu 丈夫

I

I wǒ 我
　I'm sorry Duì bù qǐ 对不起
ice bīng 冰
ice-cream bīngjílíng 冰激凌, bīngqílín 冰淇淋, xuěgāo 雪糕
if rúguǒ 如果
ill yǒubìng 有病, shēngbìng 生病
imperial huángdì de 皇帝的
　the Imperial Palace Gùgōng 故宫
inch yīngcùn 英寸
inflammation yánzhèng 炎症
information xiāoxi 消息
　information desk wènxùnchù 问讯处
injection dǎzhēn 打针
ink mòshuǐ 墨水
inn xiǎo lǚdiàn 小旅店
inside (zài) lǐmiàn (在)里面
to insure bǎoxiǎn 保险
insured letter bǎojià xìn 保价信
interesting yǒuqù 有趣,

hǎowánr 好玩儿, dàijìnr 带劲
international guójì de 国际的
interpret/interpreter kǒuyì 口译, fānyì 翻译
into dào ... lǐ 到 ... 里
introduction jièshào 介绍
Ireland Ài'ěrlán 爱尔兰
Irish Ài'ěrlán rén 爱尔兰人
to iron yùn 熨
is shì 是
it tā 它, zhè 这
its tāde 它的
itself tā zìjǐ 它自己
ivory xiàngyá 象牙
　ivory carving yádiāo 牙雕

J

jacket jiākè shān 夹克衫
jade yù 玉
　jade carving yùdiāo 玉雕
jam guǒjiàng 果酱
January yīyuè 一月
Japan Rìběn 日本
jasmine mòli huā 茉莉花
jewel bǎoshí 宝石
to join jiē 接, cānjiā 参加
journey lǚxíng 旅行
　Have a good/pleasant journey! yīlù shùnfēng! 一路顺风!
juice zhīr 汁
July qīyuè 七月
to jump tiào 跳
jumper máoyī 毛衣
June liùyuè 六月
just now gāngcái 刚才
just a minute/second děng yíxià 等一下

K

to keep bǎocún 保存, bǎochí 保持
ketchup fānqié jiàng 番茄酱
key yàoshi 钥匙
kidney bean càidòu 菜豆
kind (nice) yǒuhǎo de 友好的
　(type) zhǒng 种
kindness yǒuhǎo 友好

148

Wordlist

great kindness shèng qíng 盛情

king guówáng 国王, huángdì 皇帝

kite fēngzheng 风筝

knife xiǎodāo 小刀

to knock qiāo 敲, dǎ 打

to know zhīdao 知道, rènshi 认识, dǒng 懂

L

lacquerware qījù 漆具

lady nǚshì 女士, fūren 夫人, xiǎojie 小姐

   Ladies nǚcèsuǒ 女厕所

lamp dēng 灯

land lùdì 陆地, dì 地

   to land jiàngluò 降落

landscape fēngjǐng 风景, jǐngsè 景色

language yǔyán 语言

large dà de 大的

last shàng yīge 上一个

late wǎn 晚

later hòulái 后来

to laugh xiào 笑

laundry xǐyī fáng / diàn 洗衣房/店

lavatory cèsuǒ 厕所

laxative qīngxiè jì 轻泻剂

to learn xué(huì) 学(会)

leather pígé 皮革

   leather belt pídài 皮带

   leather shoes píxié 皮鞋

to leave for qù 去

left zuǒ (biān) de 左(边)的

leg tuǐ 腿

to lend jiè 借

less shǎo 少

letter xìn 信, zìmù 字幕

   letter box xìnxiāng 信箱

lettuce shēngcài 生菜

to lie tǎng 躺

   to lie in bed wòchuáng 卧床

life shēngmìng 生命, shēnghuó 生活

lift diàntī 电梯

to lift tái 抬

light (lamp) dēng 灯

   (adj) liàng 亮, qīng 清, qiǎn 浅

light colour qiǎnsè 浅色

lighter dǎhuǒ jī 打火机

like xiàng 象

to like ài 爱, xǐhuan 喜欢

line pái 排

lipstick kǒuhóng 口红

list biǎo 表, dān 单

to listen tīng 听

little shǎo 少, xiǎo 小

   a little yìxiē 一些, yìdiǎn 一点

   a little while yīhuìr 一会儿

live shēnghuó 生活

lobster lóngxiā 龙虾

local běndì de 本地的, běnshìde 本市的

   local train mànchē 慢车

location wèizhi 位置

lock suǒ 锁

London Lúndūn 伦敦

long cháng(jiǔ) 长(久)

   before long bùjiǔ 不久

   long distance call chángtú diànhuà 长途电话

to look kàn 看, guān 观

   to look at kàn 看

   to look for zhǎo 找

loose sōng 松, féi 肥

to lose diūshī 丢失

   to lose one's way mílù 迷路

Lost Property Office Shīwù Zhāolǐng Chù 失物招领处

loud dàshēng 大声, xiǎng 响

to love ài 爱, xǐhuan 喜欢

low dī 低

luck (hǎo)yùnqì (好)运气

luggage xíngli 行李

lunch wǔfàn 午饭

M

machine jīqì 机器

magazine zázhì 杂志

mail xìnjiàn 信件, yóujiàn 邮件

main / major zhǔyào de 主要的

to make zuò 做, zhìzào 制造, shǐ 使

make-up huàzhuāng 化装

male nánren 男人

149

Wordlist

man nánren 男人, rén 人
manager jīnglǐ 经理
to manufacture zhìzào 制造
many hěnduō 很多
map dìtú 地图
March sānyuè 三月
market shìchǎng 市场, shāngchǎng 商场
to marry jiéhūn 结婚
martial arts wǔshù 武术
massage ànmó 按摩
master shīfu 师傅, zhǔrén 主人
   to master jīngtōng 精通
match huǒchái 火柴, bǐsài 比赛
   a football match zúqiú sài 足球赛
to match xiāng pèi 相配
material bù 布, cáiliào 材料
matter shìqing 事情
   What's the matter? Chū shénme shìr le? 出什么事了?
to matter yǒu guānxi 有关系
   It doesn't matter Méi guānxi / Méi shénme 没关系/没什么
May wǔyuè 五月
may kěnéng 可能, huì 会, kěyǐ 可以
maybe dàgài 大概
me wǒ 我
meal fàn 饭
to mean yìsī shì 意思是
meat ròu 肉
meatball ròuwán 肉丸
medicine yào 药
to meet huìjiàn 会见, pèngjiàn 碰见
meeting huìyì 会议
melon guā 瓜
to mend xiūlǐ 修理
menu càidān 菜单
message kǒuxìn 口信
meter biǎo 表
metre mǐ 米
in the middle zhōngxīn 中心, zhōngděng de 中等的
midnight yèlǐ 夜里, bànyè 半夜
150 milk (niú)nǎi (牛)奶

mill gōngchǎng 工厂
million bǎiwàn 百万
   a hundred million yì 亿
mince ròuxiàn 肉馅
to mind jièyì 介意
mine wǒ de 我的
mineral water kuàngquán shuǐ 矿泉水
minor shǎo 少, xiǎo 小
minute fēn(zhōng) 分(钟)
mirror jìngzi 镜子
Miss xiǎojie 小姐
to miss diūshī 丢失
to miss a bus/train méi gǎn shàng chē 没赶上车
mistake cuòwù 错误
to misunderstand wùhuì 误会
modest qiānxū 谦虚, kèqi 客气
moist cháoshī 潮湿
moment yīhuìr 一会儿
Monday xīng qíyī 星期一
money qián 钱, kuǎn 款
   money order huìkuǎn dān 汇款单
month yuè 月
   last month shàngyuè 上月
   next month xiàyuè 下月
   this month zhège yuè 这个月
monument jìniàn bēi 纪念碑
moon yuèliang 月亮
more gèngduō 更多, gèng 更, zài 再
morning shàngwǔ 上午, zǎochén 早晨
early morning qīngchén 清晨
most zuì 最
mother mǔqīn 母亲
mountain shān 山
moustache (xiǎo)húzi (小)胡子
mouth kǒu 口, zuǐ 嘴
to move dòng 动
movie diànyǐng 电影
Mr xiānsheng 先生
Mrs fūren 夫人, tàitai 太太
Ms nǚshì 女士
much duō 多

Wordlist

museum bówùguǎn 博物馆
mushroom mógu 蘑菇
music yīnyuè 音乐
must bìxū 必须, wùbì
务必, yīnggāi 应该
my wǒ de 我的
myself wǒ zìjǐ 我自己

N

nail zhǐjia 指甲
　nail clippers zhǐjia dāo
　指甲刀
　nail polish zhǐjia yóu
　指甲油
name xìngmíng 姓名, míngzi
名字
napkin cānjīn 餐巾
nation mínzú 民族, guójiā 国
家, rénmín 人民
nationality guójí 国籍, mínzú
民族
near jìn 近
nearby fùjìn 附近
neat zhěng qí 整齐
necklace xiàngliàn 项链
to need xūyào 需要, yòng 用
　to need to (do sth.) děi 得
needle zhēn 针
negative (photo) dǐpiàn
底片
neither dōubù 都不, yěbù
也不
never cóng méiyǒu 从没有,
jué bù 决不
　never mind méi guānxi
　没关系
new xīn de 新的
　New Year xīnnián 新年
　New York Niǔyuē 纽约
　New Zealand Xīnxīlán
　新西兰
news xiāoxi 消息, xīnwén
新闻
next xià 下
　next month xiàyuè 下月
　next week xiàzhōu 下周
　next year míngnián 明年
nice hǎo 好
night yè(wǎn) 夜(晚)
　at night yèlǐ 夜里
nightgown shuìpáo 睡袍

nine jiǔ 九
nineteen shíjiǔ 十九
ninety jiǔshí 九十
no méiyǒu 没有, bù 不, bùxǔ
不许
nobody méiyǒu rén 没有人
noisy xiǎng 响
noodle miàntiáo 面条
noon zhōngwǔ 中午
nor yěbù 也不
north běi(fāng) 北(方)
northeast dōngběi 东北
northwest xīběi 西北
not bù 不
　Not at all Búyòng xiè
　不用谢, Bú kèqi 不客气
nothing méiyǒu 没有
notice-board jiēshì bǎn 揭示
板
nought líng 零
November shíyī yuè 十一月
now xiànzài 现在
number shù 数

O

o'clock diǎn(zhōng) 点钟
October shíyuè 十月
of ... de 的
office bàngōng shì 办公室
　office hours Bàngōng
　Shíjiān 办公时间
oil yóu 油
oily yóunì 油腻
OK / okay hǎo 好, xíng 行
old lǎo 老, ... suì 岁
　how old duōdà 多大, jǐsuì
　几岁
once yícì 一次, yíxià 一下
　once more zài yícì 再一次
one yī 一
　one-way ticket dānchéng
　piào 单程票
oneself zìjǐ 自己
onion yángcōng 洋葱
only jǐnjǐn 仅仅, dànshì
但是, jǐnyǒu de 仅有的
onyx mǎnǎo 玛瑙
to open kāi 开, dǎkāi 打开,
zhāngkāi 张开
opening kāi(kǒu) 开(口)
opera gējù 歌剧

operation shǒushù 手术
operator huàwùyuán 话务员,
  jiēxiàn shēng 接线生
optician yǎnjìng diàn 眼镜店
or háishì 还是, huò 或
orange júzi 桔子
  (colour) júhóng(sè)
    桔红(色)
  orange juice júzi shuǐ
    桔子水
ordinary pǔtōng 普通
other biéde 别的, duìmiàn de
    对面的, lìngwài de
    另外的
ought to yīng gāi 应该
our wǒmen de 我们的
ourselves wǒmen zìjǐ 我们自己
over zài ... shàng 在 ... 上, tài
    太
overcoat dàyī 大衣, wàitào
    外套
overseas guówài 国外
oyster háo 蚝, xián 蟓

P

package bāoguǒ 包裹
packet bāo 包, hé 盒
  a packet of cigarettes
    yī (bāo/hé) yān 一(包/盒)烟
pain téngtòng 疼痛
to paint huìhuà 绘画
painting huà 画
pair shuāng 双
  a pair of yīshuāng 一双
palace gōngdiàn 宫殿
pan píngdǐ guō 平底锅
pancake báobǐng 薄饼
pants kùzi 裤子
paper zhǐ 纸, zhèngjiàn
    证件
parcel bāoguǒ 包裹
park gōngyuán 公园
to park tíngchē 停车
  parking lot tíngchē chù
    停车处
part bùfen 部分
parting fēnfèng 分缝
party jùhuì 聚会, yànhuì
    宴会, dǎng 党
to pass jīngguò 经过, gěi 给
passport hùzhào 护照

past guò 过
paste jiànghú 浆糊
pastry diǎnxin 点心
path xiǎolù 小路
pattern shìyàng 式样
pause tíng 停
to pay fùkuǎn 付款, jiāoqián
    交钱
  to pay a bill fùzhàng 付帐
pea wāndòu 豌豆
peanut huāshēng 花生
pearl zhēnzhū 珍珠
pen gāngbǐ 钢笔
pencil qiānbǐ 铅笔
penicillin pánníxīlín 盘尼西林
people rén 人, rénmen 人们
  the people rénmín 人民
pepper hújiāo 胡椒
per měi 每
performance biǎoyǎn 表演
perfume xiāngshuǐ 香水
perhaps kěnéng 可能
perm tàngfà jīng 烫发精
permit / permission yǔnxǔ
    允许, zhǔnxǔ 准许
person rén 人
  person in charge fùzé rén
    负责人
pharmacy yàodiàn 药店
phone diànhuà 电话
  phone call diànhuà 电话
photo / photograph zhàopiàn
    照片, xiàngpiàn 相片
physical shēntǐ de 身体的
physician yīshēng 医生, dàifu
    大夫
to pick up shíqǐ 拾起
picture túhuà 图画; xiàngpiàn
    相片
  to take a picture pāizhào
    拍照, zhàoxiàng 照相
piece (yī) kuài 一块
pill yàowán 药丸, yàopiàn
    药片
pillow zhěntou 枕头
pillowcase zhěntào 枕套
pink fěnhóng (sè) 粉红(色)
pity yíhàn 遗憾
place dìfang 地方
to place fāchū 发出
  to place an order yùdìng
    预定

plane fēijī 飞机

plant zhíwù 植物; gōngchǎng 工厂

plate pánzi 盘子, diézi 碟子

platform zhàntái 站台

platinum báijīn 白金

play (xìjù) yǎnchū (戏剧) 演出, yóuxì 游戏

to play wán 玩, dǎqiú 打球, yǎnzòu 演奏

　to play basketball dǎ lánqiú 打篮球

　to play a musical instrument yǎnzòu 演奏

player yùndòngyuán 运动员, yǎnzòu zhě 演奏者

pleasant měihǎo de 美好的, yúkuài de 愉快的

please qǐng 请

pleased mǎnyì 满意, gāoxìng 高兴

plum lǐzi 李子

p.m. xiàwǔ 下午

police jǐng chá 警察, gōng' ān 公安

　police station gōng' ān jú 公安局

　policeman jǐng chá 警察

polite kèqi 客气, yǒu lǐmào 有礼貌

popular liúxíng de 流行的

porcelain cíqì 瓷器

pork zhūròu 猪肉

porridge zhōu 粥, xīfàn 稀饭

port gǎng shì 港市

porter xínglì yuán 行李员

to possess yōngyǒu 拥有

possible kěnéng de 可能的

post yóuzhèng 邮政

　post box yóutǒng 邮筒

　post card míngxìn piàn 明信片

　post office yóujú 邮局

　post and telecommunications yóudiàn 邮电

to post yóu 邮, jì 寄

postage yóufèi 邮费

pot guō 锅

potato tǔdòu 土豆, mǎlíngshǔ 马铃薯

pottery táoqì 陶器

pound sterling Yīngbàng 英镑

prawn duìxiā 对虾

to prefer gèng xǐhuan 更喜欢

to prepare / preparation zhǔnbèi 准备

present lǐwù 礼物, lǐpǐn 礼品, xiànzài 现在

president zǒngtǒng 总统, zhǔxí 主席

pretty (=nice) piàoliàng de 漂亮的

　(=very) xiāngdāng 相当

price jiàgé 价格

print (photos) xǐxiàng 洗相

to produce shēngchǎn 生产, zuò 做, zhìzào 制造, chūshì 出示

product chǎnpǐn 产品, zhìpǐn 制品

production shēngchǎn 生产, zhìzào 制造

programme jiémù dān 节目单

propose / proposal tíyì 提议, jiànyì 建议

province shěng 省

public gōnggòng de 公共的

to pull lā 拉

pullover (tàotóu) máoyī (套头) 毛衣

purple zǐ(sè) 紫(色)

purse qiánbāo 钱包

to push tuī 推

to put fàng 放

　to put sth. on chuān shàng 穿上

pyjamas shuìyī 睡衣

Q

quarter sì fēn zhī yī 四分之一

　a quarter of an hour yīkè 一刻

question wèntí 问题

to question wèn 问

queue cháng duì 长队, páiduì 排队

quick kuài 快

quiet jìng 静

quilt bèizi 被子

153

quite hěn 很, xiāngdāng 相当

R

railway tiělù 铁路
　railway station huǒchē zhàn 火车站
rain yǔ 雨
raincoat yǔyī 雨衣
rather xiāngdāng 相当
　would rather níngyuàn 宁愿
raw shēng 生
razor guā hú dāo 刮胡刀
ready zuòhǎo zhǔnbèi 做好准备, yuànyì 愿意
real/really zhēn de/zhēn de 真的/真地
receipt shōujù 收据
to receive shōudào 收到, jiēdào 接到
record jìlù 记录, chàngpiàn 唱片
red hóng (sè) 红(色)
refill bǐxīn 笔芯
refund guīhuán 归还
　to get a refund for a ticket tuìpiào 退票
registered letter guàhào xìn 挂号信
to remember jìzhù 记住
to rent zū 租
to repair xiūlǐ 修理, bǔ 补
to repay huán 还
to repeat chóngfù shuō/zuò 重复说/做
to reply dáfù 答复
to request/require yāoqiú 要求
research yánjiū 研究
reservation yùdìng 预定
to rest xiūxi 休息
　rest qíyú 其余
　to take a rest xiūxi 休息
restaurant cānguǎn 餐馆, fànguǎn 饭馆, fàndiàn 饭店
to return huán 还, huílái 回来
rice mǐ 米, fàn 饭
to ride qíchē 骑车
right (not wrong) yòu 右,

xíng 行, hǎo 好, duì 对
on the right yòubiān 右边, yòumiàn 右面
ring jièzhi 戒指
river hé 河, jiāng 江
RMB Rénmín bì 人民币
road dào 道, lù 路
roast kǎo 烤
　roast chicken shāojī 烧鸡
　roast duck kǎoyā 烤鸭
roll juǎn 卷, gǔn 滚
room fángjiān 房间, wū 屋
　a single room dānjiān 单间
round (shape) yuán de 圆的
　(direction) guǎiwān 拐弯
rubber xiàng pí 橡皮; jiāo 胶
　rubber band hóujīn tàor 猴筋儿套
ruby hóng bǎo shí 红宝石
rug xiǎo dìtǎn 小地毯
ruler géchǐ 格尺
to run pǎo 跑
　to run a fever/temperature fāshāo 发烧

S

safe (not dangerous) píng'ān 平安
　(strong box) bǎoxiǎn xiāng 保险箱
salary gōngzī 工资
sale mài 卖
　sales department ménshìbù 门市部
salt yán 盐
salty xián de 咸的
same tóngyàng de 同样的
sandal liángxié 凉鞋
sanitary wèishēng de 卫生的
sapphire lán bǎoshí 蓝宝石
satin duànzi 缎子
satisfied mǎnyì de 满意的
Saturday xīng qī liù 星期六
sauce jiàngyóu 酱油; jiàng 酱
sausage xiāngcháng 香肠
to say shuō 说, jiǎng 讲
scarf wéijīn 围巾
scene jǐngsè 景色
scenic spot míngshèng 名胜
schedule shíjiān biǎo 时间表

school xuéxiào 学校
　middle / high / secondary
　　school zhōngxué 中学
　primary school xiǎoxué
　　小学
scissors jiǎndāo 剪刀
screen píngfēng 屏风
sculpture diāosù 雕塑
sea hǎi 海; hǎiyáng
　海洋
　sea food hǎiwù 海物
to seal gàiyìn 盖印, fēng 封
seasick yūnchuán 晕船
season jìjié 季节
seat zuòwèi 座位
　take a seat zuòxià 坐下
second dì'èr 第二
second-class èr děng de
　二等的
to see kànjiàn 看见, jiànmiàn
　见面
to seize zhuā 抓
to sell mài 卖, shòu 售
semi- bàn 半
to send jì 寄; dǎfa 打发
　to send a letter jìxìn 寄信
　to send a telegram dǎ
　　diànbào 打电报
　to send one's regards to
　　xiàng ... wènhǎo 向 ...
　　问好
　to send out fā 发
September jiǔyuè 九月
seven qī 七
seventeen shíqī 十七
seventy qīshí 七十
several jǐ 几
sex xìngbié 性别
shall yào 要, jiāng 将
shampoo xǐfà jì 洗发剂
shape wàixíng 外形, yàngshì
　样式
shark shāyú 鲨鱼
　shark's fin yúchì 鱼翅
sharp zhěng 整
shaver diàndòngtìdāo 电动
　剃刀
she tā 她
sheet chuángdān 床单
ship chuán 船
shirt chènshān 衬衫
shock diànzhèn 电震

shoe xié 鞋
shoe-lace xiédài 鞋带
shop shāngdiàn 商店
short duǎn 短, ǎi 矮
shorts duǎnkù 短裤
should yīnggāi 应该; yào 要
to show chūshì 出示, zhǎnlǎn
　huì 展览会, yǎnchū 演出
shower línyù 淋浴
shrimp xiā 虾
shrine miào 庙, shéndiàn 神殿
to shut guān 关
sick yǒubìng 有病, bìng 病
side biān 边; miàn 面
sight jǐngxiàng 景象; guān 观
signature qiānmíng 签名
silk sīchóu 丝绸
silver yín 银
simple jiǎndān 简单, jiǎnpǔ
　简朴
sing / singing chànggē 唱歌
single dānrén de 单人的,
　dāngè de 单个的, dān 单
　a single ticket dānchéng
　　piào 单程票
sir xiānsheng 先生
sister jiěmèi 姐妹
sit zuò 坐
six liù 六
sixteen shíliù 十六
sixty liùshí 六十
size dàxiǎo 大小, hàomǎ
　号码
skill jìnéng 技能
skin pífū 皮肤
skirt qúnzi 裙子
sky tiānkōng 天空
sleep shuìjiào 睡觉
　sleeping berth wòpù 卧铺
　sleeping car wòpù chē 卧铺
　　车
　sleeping pill ānmián yào
　　安眠药
slides huàndēng piàn 幻灯片
slipper tuōxié 拖鞋
slow màn 慢
　slow train màn chē 慢车
slowly màn 慢
small xiǎo 小, shǎo 少
smell wèi 味
　to smell wén 闻
smile xiào 笑, wēixiào 微笑

155

Wordlist

to smoke xīyān 吸烟, chōuyān 抽烟
smoke yān 烟
snow xuě 雪
so zhèyàng 这样, nàyàng 那样
soap féizào 肥皂
soccer zúqiú 足球
society shètuán 社团
sock wàzi 袜子
soda-water qìshuǐ 汽水
soft ruǎn 软
soft-berth ticket ruǎnwò piào 软卧票
some yìxiē 一些
somebody/someone mǒurén 某人
son érzi 儿子
song gē 歌
soon hěn kuài 很快
sorry duì bùqǐ 对不起; bàoqiàn 抱歉
sound shēngyīn 声音
soup tāng 汤
sour suān 酸
south nán 南
souvenir jìniàn pǐn 纪念品
soy milk dòujiāng 豆浆
Spain xībānyá 西班牙
spareribs páigǔ 排骨
to speak shuō 说, jiǎng 讲
to spend huāqián 花钱
spinach bōcài 菠菜
spirits jiǔ 酒
to spit tǔtán 吐痰
spoon sháo 勺, chízi 匙子
sport yùndòng 运动, tǐyù 体育
sportsman/sportswoman yùndòng yuán 运动员
spring chūntiān/jì 春天/季, quán 泉
hot spring wēnquán 温泉
spring pancake chūnbǐng 春饼
spring roll chūnjuǎn 春卷
sprout yá 芽
square guǎng chǎng 广场
stadium tǐyù chǎng 体育场
stage wǔtái 舞台
stainless steel bùxiùgāng 不锈钢

stamp yóupiào 邮票
to stand zhàn 站
to stand up zhàn qǐlái 站起来
star xīng 星, míngxīng 明星
start kāishǐ 开始
state guójiā 国家
station chēzhàn 车站
stationery wénjù 文具
stationery shop wénjù diàn 文具店
stay tíngliú 停留
steel gāng 钢
stew dùn 炖, shāo 烧
stinking chòu 臭
stir-fry chǎo 炒
stocking chángtǒng wà 长统袜
stomach wèi 胃
stone shí 石; bǎoshí 宝石
to stop tíng 停
stop (bus etc) chēzhàn 车站
store shāngdiàn 商店
straight zhí 直
street jiē 街
main street dàjiē 大街
strike dǎ 打
strong qiáng(zhuàng) 强壮, láogù 牢固
student xuésheng 学生
studio zhìpiàn chǎng 制片厂
to study xuéxí 学习
style shìyàng 式样
summer xiàtiān/jì 夏天/季
sun tàiyáng 太阳
Sunday xīng qīrì 星期日
supper wǎnfàn 晚饭
sure kěndìng 肯定
surgeon (wàikē) yīshēng (外科)医生
surname xìng 姓
sweat shirt wèishēng yī 卫生衣, yùndòngyī 运动衣
sweet tián 甜
sweet and sour tángcù 糖醋, suāntián 酸甜
sweets tángguǒ 糖果
to swim yóuyǒng 游泳
swimming-pool yóuyǒng chí 游泳池
switch kāiguān 开关

Wordlist

T

table zhuōzi 桌子
table tennis pīngpāng qiú
乒乓球
to take ná 拿, qǔ 取, chī 吃
to take off qǐfēi 起飞
to take medicine fúyào
服药
to talk tánhuà 谈话; shuō 说
tall gāo 高
tap shuǐ lóngtou 水龙头
tape lùyīn dài 录音带
tape recorder lùyīn jī 录音
机
taste wèidào 味道
to taste cháng 尝
tasty hǎochī 好吃
tax shuì 税
taxi chūzū chē 出租车
tea chá 茶
to teach jiāoshū 教书
teacher lǎoshī 老师, jiàoshī
教师
team duì 队
telegram diànbào 电报
telephone diànhuà 电话
telephone directory
diànhuà hàomǎ běn 电话
号码本
television diànshì 电视
telex diànchuán 电传
to tell gàosu 告诉, jiǎng 讲
temperature wēndù 温度
temple miào 庙, sì 寺
ten shí 十
terms tiáojiàn 条件
terrible kě pà de 可怕的, hěn
huài de 很坏的
test jiǎnchá 检查, kǎoshì
考试
thanks xièxie 谢谢, gǎnxiè
感谢
that nà / nèi 那, nàge 那个
theatre xìjù 戏剧, jùyuàn
剧院
their tāmen de 他/她/它们的
them tāmen 他/她/它们
themselves tāmen zìjǐ 他/她/它
们自己
then ránhòu 然后, nàshí
那时

there nàli 那里
there is yǒu 有
there isn't méiyǒu 没有
thermometer tǐwēn jì 体温计
these zhèxiē 这些
they tāmen 他(她)
thick hòu 厚
thin báo 薄, shòu 瘦
thing dōngxi 东西
to think xiǎng 想, rènwéi
认为
third dìsān 第三
thirsty kě 渴
thirteen shísān 十三
thirty sānshí 三十
this zhè / zhèi ge 这个, jīn 今,
běn 本
those nàxiē 那些
thousand qiān 千
ten thousand wàn 万
thread xiàn 线
three sān 三
thriller jīngxiǎn piàn 惊险片
throat hóu 喉
throat lozenges hóupiàn
喉片
through guò 过, jīng 经
to throw rēng 扔
Thursday xīng qī sì 星期四
ticket piào 票
ticket office shòupiào chù
售票处
tie lǐngdài 领带
tight jǐn 紧
time shíjiān 时间, shíhou
时候, cì 次
time difference shíchā
时差
tired lèi 累, tián 田累
toast kǎo miànbāo 烤面包
to toast wèi … gānbēi 为 …
干杯
today jīntiān 今天
together (zài) yìqǐ 在一起
toilet cèsuǒ 厕所
toilet paper wèishēng zhǐ
卫生纸
tomato xīhóng shì 西红柿
tomato ketchup fānqié
jiàng 蕃茄酱
tomb fén 坟, mù 墓
tomorrow míngtiān 明天

Wordlist

tone yīndiào 音调, shēng 声
too yě 也, tài 太
tooth/teeth yá 牙
   toothbrush yáshuā 牙刷
   toothpaste yágāo 牙膏
   toothpick yáqiān 牙签
total quán 全
to touch pèng 碰, chùmō
   触摸, dòng 动
tough yìng 硬
tour lǚxíng 旅行, lǚyóu
   旅游
tourist lǚyóu zhě 旅游者
towards xiàng 向, wǎng 往
towel máojīn 毛巾
town chéngzhèn 城镇
toy wánjù 玩具
trade mǎimài 买卖
traditional chuántǒng de
   传统的
train huǒchē 火车
translate/translator fānyì
   翻译
to travel lǚxíng 旅行, cānguān
   参观
traveller lǚxíng zhě 旅行者
   traveller's cheque lǚxíng
   zhīpiào 旅行支票
tray tuōpán 托盘
tree shù 树
trip lǚxíng 旅行
trouble máfan 麻烦; bìng 病
trousers kùzi 裤子
truck kǎchē 卡车
true zhēn de 真的; duì de
   对的
to try chángshì 尝试
   to try to find zhǎo 找
T shirt tīxù shān T恤衫
Tuesday xīng qī'èr 星期二
to turn wān 弯, zhuǎn 转
   to turn off guān 关
   to turn on kāi 开
turquoise lǜsōng shí 绿松石
twelve shí'èr 十二
twenty èrshí 二十
twice liǎngcì 两次; liǎngbèi
   两倍
two èr 二; liǎng 两
type zhǒnglèi 种类
   to type dǎzì 打字
typewriter dǎzì jī 打字机

U

unable bùnéng 不能, búhuì
   不会
under zài ... xià 在 ...下
underclothes chènyī 衬衣
underground dìtiě 地铁
underpants chènkù 衬裤
to understand míngbái 明白,
   dǒng 懂, zhīdào 知道
underwear chènyī 衬衣
university dàxué 大学
up xiàng shàng 向上
upstairs lóushàng 楼上
urgent jǐnjí 紧急
us wǒmén 我们
US dollar Měiyuán 美元
to use shǐyòng 使用
useful yǒuyòng 有用

V

vacant kōng 空
vacation jiàqī 假期
valuables guìzhòng wùpǐn
   贵重物品
vase huāpíng 花瓶
vegetable cài 菜
vegetarian chīsù zhě 吃素者
very hěn 很, tài 太
view jǐngsè 景色, guāndiǎn
   观点
village xiāngcūn 乡村
vinegar cù 醋
visa qiānzhèng 签证
visit cānguān 参观, fǎngwèn
   访问
visitor láibīn 来宾
voice shēngyīn 声音

W

wage gōngzī 工资
waist yāo 腰
to wait děng 等
waiting-room hòuchē shì
   候车室, hòují shì 候机室
waitress (nǚ) fúwù yuán
   (女)服务员
to wake up xíng 醒
walk zǒu 走, sànbù 散步
wall qiáng 墙
wallet qiánbāo 钱包
to want yào 要, xūyào 需要

158

to want to xiǎngyào 想要

warm nuǎnhuo 暖和

to wash xǐ 洗

   to wash clothes xǐ yīfu
   洗衣服

   to wash one's hands xǐshǒu
   洗手

washing-machine xǐyī jī
   洗衣机

washing-powder xǐyī fěn
   洗衣粉

watch biǎo 表

   to watch kàn 看

water shuǐ 水

wave bōlàng 波浪

way lù 路, dào 道

WC cèsuǒ 厕所

we wǒmen 我们

to wear chuān 穿, dài 戴

weather tiānqì 天气

Wednesday xīngqī sān 星期三

week xīngqī 星期, zhōu 周

weekend zhōumò 周末

weight zhòngliàng 重量

welcome huānyíng 欢迎

   you're welcome búyào kèqi
   不要客气, búyòngxiè 不用
   谢

well hǎo 好

well-known yǒumíngde
   有名的

west xī 西

western xīfāng de 西方的

wet shī de 湿的, cháo de
   潮的

what shénme 什么

   what date jǐhào 几号

   what number jǐhào 几号

   what time jǐdiǎn 几点

when (shēnme) shíhou (什么)
   时候

where zài nǎli 在哪里, nǎr
   哪儿

whether shìfǒu 是否

which nǎge 哪个

while yīhuìr 一会儿

whisky wēishìjì 威士忌

white bái(sè) 白(色)

who shéi / shuí 谁

whole quán de 全的

whose shéi / shuí de 谁的

why wèi shénme 为什么

wide kuān 宽, guǎng 广

wife àiren 爱人, qīzi 妻子

willow liǔshù 柳树

to win yíng 赢

wind fēng 风

wine (pútao) jiǔ (葡萄)酒

winter dōngtiān / jì 冬天/季

wire diànxiàn 电线

wish xīwàng 希望

with hé 和, jùyǒu 具有

without méiyǒu 没有

woman fùnǚ 妇女, nǚrén
   女人

wonderful hǎo jí le 好极了,
   dàijìn 带劲

wood mù 木

woollen máo de 毛的

word huà 话, zì 字

work gōngzuò 工作

world shìjiè 世界

worth jiàzhí 价值

would like to xiǎng yào
   想要

to wrap bāo 包

to write xiě 写, jì 记

wrong búduì 不对, cuò 错,
   huài le 坏了

X

x-ray àikèsī guāng 爱克斯光

Y

year nián 年

   years niándài 年代

   last year qùnián 去年

   next year míngnián 明年

   this year jīnnián 今年

   ... years old ... suì 岁

yellow huáng(sè) 黄(色)

yes duì 对, shì 是

yesterday zuótiān 昨天

yoghurt suānnǎi 酸奶

you (informal) nǐ 你, nǐmen
   你们

   (formal) nín 您

young niánqīng de 年轻的,
   xiǎo de 小的

younger nián xiǎo de 年小的

   younger brother dìdi
   弟弟

younger sister mèimei 妹妹
your nǐ de 你的, nǐmén de 你们的
yourself nǐ zìjǐ 你自己
youth qīngnián 青年

Z

zero líng 零
    below zero língxià 零下
zipper lāsuǒr 拉锁
zoo dòngwù yuán 动物园